D1532381

Empowering Green Initiatives with IT

Empowering Green Initiatives with IT

A STRATEGY AND IMPLEMENTATION GUIDE

Carl H. Speshock

WILEY

John Wiley & Sons, Inc.

Library of Congress Cataloging-in-Publication Data:
Speshock, Carl H.
   Empowering green initiatives with IT : a strategy and implementation guide / Carl Speshock.
      p. cm.
   Includes bibliographical references and index.
   ISBN 978-0-470-58752-2 (hardback); 978-0-470-90647-7 (ebk);
978-0-470-90648-4 (ebk); 978-0-470-90649-1 (ebk)
   1. Data processing service centers—Energy conservation.   2. Information technology—Environmental aspects.   3. Green technology—Data processing.   4. Social responsibility of business.   I. Title.
   TJ163.5.O35S64 2010
   658.4'083—dc22

                                                            2010018595

Printed in the United States of America
10 9 8 7 6 5 4 3 2 1

To my wife Angie, son Joshua, and daughter Cassandra who have offered support and encouragement.

Hoping the global efforts of environmental sustainability through productive, responsible, and effective Green initiatives will jointly benefit the citizens and environment of the planet.

Contents

Preface

Green initiatives to achieve environmental sustainability have become mainstream topics of discussion in the business, consumer, and government sectors. There are many contributing factors, some with more visibility and emphasis than others. One factor is that world and political leaders have increased their participation and involvement in global warming projects and regulations. This has created demand for environmentally sustainable policies to be strategized and Green initiatives to be planned, developed, and implemented. Organizations need to shift to a more customer-oriented focus to increase their competitiveness, comply with governmental regulations, decrease operational costs, and project themselves as being more environmentally friendly and socially responsible besides satisfying consumer demands by being more eco-friendly.

Furthermore, it is becoming more necessary for businesses and organizations to implement Green initiatives due to the increases in demand for energy sources, global warming effects, customer pressure, and the need to reduce carbon footprints and emissions. According to the U.S. Environmental Protection Agency, market trends suggest that the demand for energy resources will rise dramatically over the next 25 years. Global demand for all energy sources is forecast to grow by 57%; U.S. demand for all types of energy is expected to increase by 31% by 2030; electricity demand in the United States will grow by at least 40% by 2032; and new power generation equal to nearly 300 1000-megawatt power plants will be needed to meet electricity demand by 2030.[1]

The next graph displays U.S. energy consumption by different fuel types with current and projected usages.[2] This graph allows for comparison of Green and carbon-emitting energy sources, as well as their projected consumption values over the next few decades. Much needs to be done to alter the consumption values more in favor of Green energy sources.

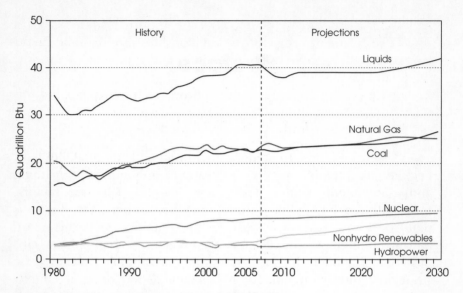

U.S. Energy Consumption by Fuel (1980–2030)
Source: United States Department of Energy, Energy Information Administration.

What does this all mean for businesses? If demand outstrips supply, as was the case in 2008 across the globe, energy prices can rise to record levels, thus substantially impacting business activities. This could lead to reduced profits due to high operating costs, decline of sales of energy-using products and services, loss of competitiveness, market reductions and disruptions due to reduction in demand and supply chain instabilities, and most noticeably a recession of great magnitude and length.

Thus, it is in the best interest of an organization to reduce its energy needs and shift to using energy from renewable energy sources. This could be one goal of the organization's overall environmentally sustainable policy and strategy. Doing this will require the assistance of as many of the organization's resources as possible to maximize the value and potential of Green-related initiatives. One such organizational resource is the information technology (IT) department.

Green initiative efforts with the IT department build on the strategic IT-business relationship that should exist within organizations. This relationship has a mission to strategically enhance an organization's profitability, productivity, efficiency, competitiveness, and compliance, and positively affect many other strategic goals. The IT department brings to the relationship resources and knowledge; thus it can contribute capabilities and functionality to assist an organization with its Green initiatives. Furthermore, many Green initiatives require computer and network technology, application software, Web sites, and the like—the purview of the IT department.

In a U.S.-based study AMR Research conducted in April 2006,[3] environmental initiatives played second fiddle to social programs such as education outreach, scholarships, and volunteerism. European research, however, yielded quite different results. IT-related spending on environmental initiatives is higher than previously thought. Results of an AMR Research survey of 200 European companies across the United Kingdom, Germany, the Netherlands, and Spain identify that the total technology-related spending on environmental initiatives would exceed 21% of total IT spending in 2007 (once personnel, auditing, and compliance costs are included). Spending is expected to increase dramatically in coming years as increasing numbers of companies seek to ensure that their supply partners (and even customers) conform to modern thinking

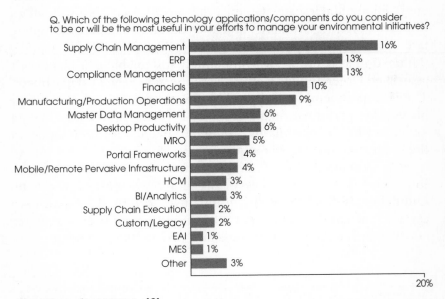

Q. Which of the following technology applications/components do you consider to be or will be the most useful in your efforts to manage your environmental initiatives?

Supply Chain Management	16%
ERP	13%
Compliance Management	13%
Financials	10%
Manufacturing/Production Operations	9%
Master Data Management	6%
Desktop Productivity	6%
MRO	5%
Portal Frameworks	4%
Mobile/Remote Pervasive Infrastructure	4%
HCM	3%
BI/Analytics	3%
Supply Chain Execution	2%
Custom/Legacy	2%
EAI	1%
MES	1%
Other	3%

Percentage of responses, n = 191

Technologies for Environmental Initiatives—Percentage of IT Budget
Source: AMR Research, 2006.

regarding sustainability, boycotting those that ignore the issue. Environmental initiatives are also becoming a board-driven issue, having languished at an operational level for too long. As shown in the previous graphic, survey respondents found that specific technologies were beneficial in assisting their organization's environmental initiatives.

Green initiatives with the IT department can be viewed in stages. The next graphic shows the six stages that can benefit the utilization and integration of the IT department into Green initiatives that will assist an organization in achieving their overall environmentally sustainable goals. The six stages reflect the establishment of having benefits and drivers defined that reflect positive mentions of IT department involvement in Green initiatives. From here, the organizations will do a deep dive into the many human and technical resources and IT offerings that can contribute to the Green initiatives. The next two stages create the strategy and plan using disciplined approaches and concepts that are backed up by standards, best practices, software tools, and regulatory compliance requirements. The organization implements the plan by taking the environmentally sustainable goals, objectives, and their associated actions and creates Green initiative projects that will assign resources, offerings, funding, timelines, and much more to complete tasks and fulfill the project's objectives. Wrapping up the stages is the need to assess your environmentally sustainable goals and their associated Green initiative efforts with the aid of the IT department. The IT department can assist with monitoring, reporting, and assessing goal key performance indicators (KPIs), statuses, risks, and budget amounts with the granularity and details needed for each aspect of the organization's assessment needs.

The strength and level of alignment of the IT-business relationship is essential for the success of Green initiatives. Strategic organizational goals should view Green initiatives with the IT department as essential and of value, not as nonproductive overhead costs, efforts that reduce competeveness and profitability; rather they are

Green Initiative Stages with the IT Department

the opposite. Forces outside the organization demand and require that it produce Greener products and services and reduce its operational carbon footprint; here Green initiatives with the IT department become part of an organization's strategic goals. Thus, the IT department offerings are incorporated into the efforts through the strategic IT-business relationship. One such example is related to energy efficiency becoming more of a corporate initiative; IT departments likely will be heavily involved in leading enterprise initiatives to improve energy use while reducing the corporate carbon footprint. Businesses that sell Green technologies and services (i.e., solar and wind energy systems, fuel cells, data center cooling, and power systems) would utilize IT department offerings in a manner directly related to the engineering, manufacture, and sale of these product and service offering to Green consumers. As mentioned throughout this book, you don't have to be a Green technology manufacturer or service business to benefit from IT department offerings to assist with specific Green initiatives.

The benefits of integrating the IT department with an organization's Green initiatives are straightforward and obvious. Enterprise operations and technology implementations of many IT departments span the entire corporation and can create cross-functional relationships. IT projects also interface with many different business units and have global interactions and experiences. IT operations typically interact globally with many employees through the IT department's help desk. These are examples of why there should be no doubt in utilizing the IT department with your organization's Green initiatives. The benefits can be from the IT department's integration with many organizational units and possessing deep business process interaction and organizational interconnectivity experiences.

How to Use This Book

This book focuses on the benefits to be gained by strategizing, planning, and implementing Green initiatives with the IT department. Furthermore, it offers insight into assessing Green IT initiatives via the use of business intelligence dashboards and Balanced Scorecards that can assist organizations to analyze KPIs related to their Green initiative projects and efforts.

This book is written as a guidebook for both nontechnical and technical persons who may or may not be in the IT field. The audience includes chief executives, IT executives and management, business and IT students, IT architects, project managers, business planners and strategists, environmental strategists, environmental regulators, and many more. The book discusses Green initiative efforts that assist with an organization's overall environmental sustainability policy and goals that relate to the private and public sectors, as well as with those in academia.

Those benefiting from this book could be performing research, strategizing Green initiatives of strategic value, and/or beginning or well into a Green initiative planning, strategy, and/or implementation effort. The book offers something to all who are influenced or participating at some level with Green initiatives.

Chapter Organization

The book is broken down into chapters and appendixes that group and relate information that is in alignment with Green initiative stages with the integration of the IT department shown in the previous graphic. The appendixes are resources that offer templates for guidance in your organization's Green initiative efforts.

Chapter 1: Green Initiative Drivers and Benefits with IT highlights the drivers that lead organizations to pursue Green initiative projects. These drivers are a culmination of internal and external forces. The mutual benefits to be gained with the Green initiative–IT relationship are discussed. The IT-business relationship is of strategic value because of the capabilities and functionality that the IT department has that can assist an organization with its Green initiatives. Furthermore, the IT department can satisfy the needs of many Green initiatives for computer and network technology, application software, Web sites, and so on. It is the strength and the level of alignment of the IT-business relationship that is essential for the success of Green initiatives.

Chapter 2: IT Resources and Offerings to Assist Green Initiatives discusses in detail the IT department's resources and offerings. These can include human and technical resources, application development, IT research, partnerships, and vendors that can assist with Green initiatives. It is here that the reader can visualize much of what is available to Green initiative efforts from the organization's IT department. One such example is with offerings, for they are categorized into two types: general and specific. General IT department offerings are typical across many organizations and include:

- Previous knowledge and experience in Green initiatives
- Positioned as a strategic partner within organizations
- User and implementer of technology (i.e., network, server, data center, application, etc.)
- Green initiative technology implementers (i.e., video teleconferencing, server and disk storage virtualization, business applications)

IT department offerings that are more specific to assisting with Green initiatives include:

- Green IT advising
- IT data center design and engineering that could assist Green building strategies and reduce an organization's energy consumption
- IT department–created dashboard and Balanced Scorecards with Green-initiative KPIs from IT application development efforts
- Deployment of a third-party custom application from the IT department to specifically support Green initiatives
- IT department–created collaborative portals for Green initiative content and collaboration

Chapter 3: Green Initiative Strategy with IT builds on the strategic IT-business relationship, organizational structure, and strategic planning. It is not a strategy that is to be implemented for one business quarter to affect the bottom line immediately, attract stock purchasers, and then discard. Furthermore, Green initiatives are not to be planned at a department or project level but must be part of an organization's strategic planning and in alignment with its strategic goals. One such strategy concept would be to create organizational changes that consider structure, processes, and funding priorities as they relate to changes in implementing Green initiatives that are of strategic value. A more granular example of an organizational structure change could be the implementation of an executive position on par with CEO, CIO, CTO, and CFO. Doing this would emphasize Green initiatives at the corporate level and allow for executive interaction for the CIO who represents the IT department.

Strategy mapping is a tool that can be used to assist with this stage. This technique offers a visual representation of the links among the different components of a strategy.

Chapter 4: Green Initiative Planning with IT offers in-depth information on planning concepts and processes that could be utilized to integrate the IT department into the overall environmental sustainability plan in an effective and productive manner. Green initiative planning with the end goal of environmental sustainability for the organization incorporates a long-term strategy that is of strategic business value, has processes and flow, has flexibility, and is dynamic. With the use of the environmental management system (EMS), the planning process framework integrates the IT department in a way that will substantially benefit the planning phase and processes with the department's resources and offerings.

Chapter 5: Green Initiative Implementation with IT offers insight into the process of implementing Green initiatives with IT departmental resources and offerings during project definition and implementation. The chapter discusses the integration of IT resources and offerings at certain stages of the implementation process and how the IT department can be effectively engaged within the implementation process. Team unity and collaboration among IT and non-IT personnel throughout implementation is mentioned as well.

The continued use of the EMS during the implementation stage and the introduction of project management will be presented to be exposed to effective and disciplined project management concepts that will effectively assist in the implementation of Green initiative projects. Productive and effective project management is the key to successful implementation of the Green initiative actions necessary to meet environmentally sustainable goals and objectives.

Chapter 6: Green Initiative Assessment with IT offers insight into how to assess your Green initiatives with respect to the overall environmentally sustainable goals and strategic goals of enhancing social responsibility, customer satisfaction, and competiveness with the aid of IT technology and offerings. Such offerings include the use of Balanced Scorecards displaying KPIs and dashboards, reports, data mining tools, and much more.

Assessment will be led by the organization's assessment team comprised of representatives from within its business functions and specific to the process of assessing the completion of Green-related objectives in relation to meeting the overall strategic business goal of environmental sustainability. The assessment process will include audits, research, stakeholder and customer feedback surveys, and other tools and processes that will provide insight into analyzing the return on investment of the organization's Green initiative efforts.

The appendixes include resource links and listings, Green initiative planning, and an implementation checklist. They can be used to complement and assist an organization's Green initiative efforts by offering sample templates for reviewing the components of the planning and implementation stages of those efforts. A glossary is also included.

The chapters and appendixes can be read and used in sequence or the reader can jump to a particular point in the book pertinent to needs and desires. The book is in alignment with current and potential efforts of Green initiatives within organizations.

Notes

1. Annual Energy Outlook (DOE/EIA-0383(2007)), "International Energy Outlook 2007"; (DOE/EIA-0484(2007)), "Inventory of U.S. Greenhouse Gas Emissions and Sinks: 1990–2005," April 2007 (EPA 430-R-07-002).
2. Ibid.
3. www.amrresearch.com/Content/View.aspx?pmillid=19941

Empowering Green Initiatives with IT

1

Green Initiative Drivers and Benefits with IT

More than ever before, Green initiatives are becoming mainstream topics that are of strategic value for an organization and its customers. For this reason, it is crucial that Green initiatives are strategized in a way that creates benefits across the board. There are governmental, organizational, consumer focused, and ethical drivers that are fueling the Green initiative movement, and these drivers should be strategically evaluated to determine placement in assisting with achieving strategic organizational goals that benefit an organization's profitability, competitiveness, and consumer satisfaction rating.

Green initiatives are not a short-term, low-impact, scratch-the-surface effort. Adopting Green initiatives requires an organization to make long-term substantial changes in strategic thinking, employee and consumer relations, and daily operations. Green initiatives need to have a long-term orientation that does not focus solely on quarterly earnings to please short-term investors. Additionally, a short-term perspective also hinders innovation and research and development, diminishes investment in human capital, encourages financial gymnastics, and discourages leadership.[1]

Furthermore, Green initiatives require an organization to be transparent, socially responsible, ethical, and compliant with striving to increase environmental sustainability. Much planning, dedication, responsibility, and commitment needs to be put forth with Green initiatives to show both your employees and consumers that your goals and level of commitment are sincere, long term, trusting, and truly environmentally friendly.

Understanding that Green initiatives need to be strategically planned and implemented, an organization will reach out to its strengths and resources to assist the effort. One such valuable resource is the Information Technology (IT) department. The IT resources, both human and technical, along with its experience in working across business functions, can assist substantially in productive and effective planning and implementation of Green initiatives. This fact is substantiated in Figure 1.1, which shows that Green initiatives are a summation of:

Driving Forces + IT Department Offerings + Organizational Strategic Goals = Green Initiatives Benefits and Drivers with IT Department

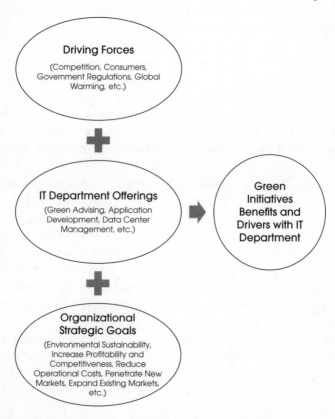

Figure 1.1   Components for Strategic Green Initiatives

Drivers for Green Initiatives

Green initiatives are becoming more of a necessity for businesses and organizations due to the increases in demand for energy sources, global warming effects, customer pressure, and the need to reduce carbon footprints and emissions due to governmental regulations and tax credits. According to the United States Environmental Protection Agency (EPA), market trends suggest that the demand for energy resources will rise dramatically over the next 25 years; in fact, global demand for all energy sources is forecast to grow by 57%, U.S. demand for all types of energy is expected to increase by 31% by 2030, 56% of the world's energy use will be in Asia, electricity demand in the United States will grow by at least 40% by 2032, and new power generation equal to nearly 300 1000-megawatt power plants will be needed to meet electricity demand by 2030.[2]

Figure 1.2 shows world energy use by different fuel types with current and projected usages. This graph allows for comparison of Green and carbon-emitting energy sources (coal, oil, etc., as well as their projected consumption values over the next few decades. Much needs to be done to alter the consumption values more in favor of

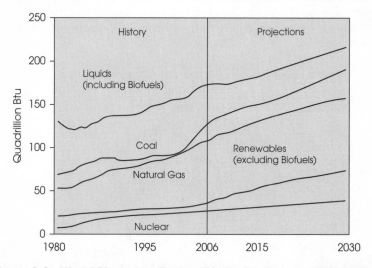

Figure 1.2   World Marketed Energy Use by Fuel Type (1980–2030)
Source: Energy Information Agency, "International Energy Outlook Report" (March 2009)

Green energy sources to assist with reductions in greenhouse gases, carbon footprints, and global warming.

What does this all mean for businesses? If energy demand outstrips energy supply, as was the case in 2008 across the globe, energy prices can rise to record levels, substantially impacting business activities. This could lead to reduced profits due to high operating costs, decline of sales of energy-using products and services, loss of competitiveness, market reductions and disruptions due to reduction in demand and supply chain instabilities, and, most noticeably, a recession of great magnitude and length. Thus, it is in the best interest of an organization to reduce its energy needs. Doing so would reduce the influence of rising energy costs; it also has the additional benefit of assisting in the Green movement sweeping the planet that is striving to limit the effects of global warming and climate change.

Figure 1.3 offers insight into the many different types of drivers that can initiate, sustain, and influence Green initiatives. The types and range of these drivers are wide ranging but are interrelated in a manner that coincides with the efforts of Green initiatives. Green initiatives are to be planned at the strategic level of an organization and with the organization as whole. Furthermore, the initiatives take into account external and internal aspects of the organization's business goals and processes.

Let's take all of the components in Figure 1.3 and examine an example of how they are interrelated in a sample manufacturing-type organization, to see the benefits of the Green initiative drivers.

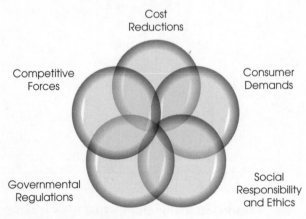

Figure 1.3   Green Initiative Drivers

Driver-Interrelated Example

Consumers demand that manufacturing of an organization's products be Green certified via compliance with national and international certification programs as well as be in compliance with United Nations and national and local governmental regulations and/or recommendations. The shift in eco-friendly manufacturing has allowed for implementation of newer manufacturing technology and processes that are much more energy and process efficient, thus becoming environmentally friendly and offering a reduction in costs. The reduction in operating costs and the production of products that are more in alignment with Green consumer demands enhance the organization's ability to deal with competitive forces in the Green economy. To cap this off, the organization adds another feather to its social responsibility cap by becoming a business that is more eco-friendly.

Social Responsibility and Ethical Practices

Green consumer movements are demanding that organizations enhance their socially responsible and ethical business practices across the board, both internal and external to the organization. Green consumers are requesting that Green initiatives have strong social and ethical components with these characteristics:

- Transparent
- Genuine
- Audited
- Reported
- Internally oriented
- Externally orientated
- Legal and legitimate

Acting socially responsible is more than a best practice recommendation for organizations; it is an external and internal business regulation specific to ethical, social, and environmental concerns that is to be enforced and engrained in the organization's business model and strategic goals. It reflects a sincere, genuine, and deliberate effort that combines serious consideration of others, the environment, and the community with effective actions.

Many organizations currently have and are creating codes of ethics that relate to social, economic, and environmental relevance. For example, the first principle of the code of ethics of the International Society for Performance Improvement is: "Strive to conduct yourself, and manage your projects and their results, in ways that add value for your clients, their customers, and the global environment."[3]

Increasing your organization's level of social responsibility can offer substantial benefits in customer satisfaction and sales and a reduction in governmental fines and infringements. Gaining the public's trust that your Green initiatives are truly offering socially responsible benefits is a win-win effort. In contrast, those who are deceitful, misleading, and conspicuous in their efforts to become more socially responsible will be exposed. This deceit will affect not only the organization's relationship with its customers but also with its investors and governmental regulators.

Walk the walk, don't talk the talk! Offer transparency to the public in your Green initiative efforts, goals, and mission. Although the release of trade secrets is not beneficial to an organization's competitiveness, there is still quite a bit of information that can be communicated to the public for your Green initiative efforts to be viewed as credible. Communication can be done in the form of a Web site, stockholder meetings, advertisements, trade magazine articles, corporate reporting, and much more. Holding back on Green initiative information can be as counterproductive as touting efforts that are seen as lacking any real value to Green consumers and the environment. Additionally, having your Green initiative efforts audited, certified, and validated by external entities offers additional credibility to your standing and level of social responsibility, besides making you more transparent to Green consumers, investors, creditors, and governmental regulators.

To view socially responsible acts as a burden on the profitability and competitiveness of your organization is not going to win you Green consumers; instead, it will create dissatisfied consumers. As is often pointed out, a happy customer will come back, but a disgruntled customer will tell others about his or her dissatisfaction with the company and discourage friends from dealing with it.[4] Green consumers view socially responsible organizations as those that understand that the bottom line is a composite of wins for the environment, their employees, the community, and profitability—not *just* profitability.

Social responsibility is being more than Green on the surface. If your Green label is comparable to surface makeup that can be rubbed off and has to be touched up to continue to project this Green made-up look, you are participating in the practice of greenwashing. Green consumers want to see socially responsible organizations that are Green throughout. They look for practices that reflect Green integration from top to bottom, throughout the organization fabric, not just on the surface. Greenwashing is a marketing ploy that strives to establish an eco-friendly image to consumers, investors, and governmental regulators. Organizations that practice this deceitful and unethical business practice are following a destructive and counterproductive path of business operations. Green consumers will expose the scam of the organization's manipulation and selfishness to protect its own image over the selfless act of achieving high levels of customer satisfaction by assisting with the world's environmental challenges. Many watchdog groups (i.e., Corpwatch and Greenpeace) are monitoring Greenwashing, offering Green consumers a source for the latest information on organizations participating in greenwashing tactics.

Greenwash

The act of misleading consumers regarding the environmental practices of a company or the environmental benefits of a product or service.

Source: Greenpeace. "Greenwashing," www.stopgreenwash.org/, 2009.

Being sincere, genuine, and dedicated to socially responsible acts that will productively address climate change and greenhouse gases is an attitude that is projected from the top. Leadership within the organization's executive ranks, governmental leaders of nation-states, the United Nations (UN) headquarters, and other key decision groups need to be clear, decisive, and vocal in their Green initiative efforts in order to be viewed as effective leaders for Green citizens of the world. If organizational leadership is viewed as indecisive, careless, ineffective, and deceitful in its Green initiative decisions and actions, Green consumers, competitors, and regulators may consider that the organization is practicing Greenwashing tactics. An organization can choose to take the path of ineffective governmental leadership, i.e., not complying with UN environmental sustainability polices, nonexistent government-offered environment initiatives and subsidies, etc., and independently pursue to implement effective Green initiatives by itself. This has been the case for many organizations who look towards government for leadership and assistance, but what is more effective is public and private sector leadership alignment, collaboration, and partnership of Green initiatives.

Green consumers are not only demanding that national and local governments, the UN, and citizens of the world join together to increase socially responsible acts and ethical practices, they are demanding that organizations do it voluntarily and sincerely, showing effective gains year after year of participation and involvement. If your organization becomes more socially responsible and ethical in its business activities due merely to regulations and laws, Green consumers will see you as insincere in your efforts. Let's compare this to how consumers watched organization responses to the Sarbanes-Oxley (SOX) Act and took note of those that took minimal actions and those that went beyond the SOX minimum requirements. This will also be the case with Green consumers watching organizations complying with environmental regulations and environmental sustainability policies; thus, this is an alert to organizations that want to do only what is required of them and no more.

What are some types of socially responsible and ethical practices that are related to Green initiatives? The Microsoft Corporation has been at the forefront of social responsibility through its commitment to reduce the impact of its operations and products and to become a leader in environmental responsibility. Microsoft created and manages its own transportation bus system for campus commuters who found that public transportation was not satisfying their needs; thus, the company created one of the world's largest private bus systems.[5] This private transportation system also reduces employees' carbon emissions. Many metropolitan areas lack adequate and environmentally friendly transportation systems for their taxpaying citizens; here is a private company taking money from its profits to implement a socially responsible program to reduce its carbon footprint. This is an example of an ethical business practice that returns profits to benefit employees and the local community.

Partnering with Eco-Friendly Organizations   Further expanding on corporate socially responsible involvement is the forming of a partnership with eco-friendly and -oriented profit and nonprofit organizations. One such example is McDonald's Corporation's partnership with the Environmental Defense Fund (EDF). McDonald's and the EDF have been working since 1989 on joint projects that have achieved some major environmental milestones. McDonald's has strived to build on this partnership and to continue to set goals that will reduce energy usage in its restaurants.[6] Wal-Mart and the EDF also have a partnership focused on reducing the carbon footprint of the world's largest retailer and improving environmental sustainability.

Corporations that form partnerships with eco-friendly organizations can add credibility to their Green initiative efforts and show Green consumers their commitment to addressing environmental challenges. A few eco-friendly organizations are:

- EarthFirst!
- Environmental Defense Fund
- Greenpeace
- National Audubon Society
- National Resources Defense Council
- National Wildlife Federation
- Rainforest Action Network
- Sierra Club
- World Wildlife Fund

Web portals, directories, and listings can assist organizations in finding a nonprofit organization to partner with. A few examples:

- EcoEarth.Info: www.ecoearth.info
- Go Green Hampton Roads.com: http://gogreenhamptonroads .com/

Employees of Socially Responsible Organizations   Employees are eager to assist with the Greening of their organizations. Many recycling and energy conservation efforts have been implemented within organizations. In this century, Green initiatives and existing eco-friendly programs will be scaled out across the whole organizations to encompass more, if not all, aspects of business operations. By increasing your eco-friendly efforts, the company will benefit from:

- Productivity increases
- Retention increases
- Healthier employees
- More engaged and involved employees
- Ability to attract better talent

Employees will be more satisfied with their jobs and their employer, and will feel positive and proud about the work that they do.

Employees can be motivated when their organization becomes more socially responsible. Going to work for an organization that inflicts great harm to the environment, the community, and its employees is not a motivation stimulator. This increase in motivation from being eco-friendly sets the stage for more positive and proud employees. When their organization is positively affecting the community, employees, and others' well-being, and making great strides in reducing its carbon footprint, employees exhibit a sense of pride. This pride is increased in those workers who enjoy participating and being engaged in Green initiatives; they feel the direct impact of their benefits to the Green challenges we are confronting.

Offering a work environment that is safe, healthy, and eco-friendly is a win-win for the welfare and effectiveness of employees and the organization's socially responsible efforts. When an organization makes the effort to implement Green initiatives that directly affect employees, those employees recognize that their employer is genuinely concerned about their welfare. Implementing healthier work conditions via eco-friendly building changes (i.e., better air filtering, enhanced landscaping and green areas for employees to take breaks, chemical usage that is more eco-friendly and employee-friendly, etc.) motivates and stimulates employees to be more productive. This can become a hiring and retention benefit for the organization. Employees seem to stay on longer when they feel the employer is looking out for them. This is a selling point for the organization for potential new hires. Current college graduates are very much in tune with the environmental challenges and those organizations that have the greatest levels of participation in Green initiatives.

Cost Reductions

Reducing organizational costs have become a mainstream theme for many in both the private and public sector around the globe. Due to the global recession that took hold in 2009, leading to reductions in sales, profits, tax revenue, and many other sources for organizational budgets, the need to reduce costs is a must to stay competitive and to stay on or under budget. Cost reductions are a key driver for Green initiatives if the cost savings are substantial, can carry for an extended period of time, can be managed effectively, and are in alignment with strategic objectives of the organization. So, how exactly can Green initiatives assist with this organizational requirement? Let's look at one area where Green initiatives can reduce operational costs, thus possibly reducing overall organizational costs.

Operationally, organizations can strive to reduce their energy consumption costs (i.e., heating/cooling, lights, computer equipment, data centers, trucking/delivery fuel, etc.). This type of operational-related Green initiative could yield both short- and long-term cost reductions. Changes in power management settings and adjustments for computer desktops and servers could immediately reduce power consumption, reductions in the number of computer servers in a data center with the use of server visualization technologies could reduce overall data center power consumption and custom IT applications that tracked delivery truck routes and fuel costs and dynamically adjusted for more efficient routes, etc.

Many times Green initiatives are implemented only if they save money and/or establish compliance with a regulatory requirement. Will this trend be the norm, or are there any exceptions? Is it acceptable for a Green initiative to offer no immediate organizational cost reductions but increase the organization's level of social responsibility or penetrate a new market that may increase sales in the near future? Green initiatives often require financing up front for planning and then implementation; thus, organizations may view Green initiatives as an unnecessary funding need during tough economic times. Those in decision-making positions may require more documentation than positive returns on investment and possible cost reductions verified and backed up with examples. Changing their minds may require adding to the mention of cost reductions the facts of positive increases in the organization's socially responsible image, establishment of Green product and service offerings that will attract Green consumers, and offering an edge on the competition if this effort places you in the leader position. To offset costs and possibly to achieve the required level of organizational cost reductions for your Green initiative efforts, you can seek government subsidies, tax credits, grants, and low-interest business loans.

The reality is that being mindful of the environment does not have to be challenging from a cost-savings or implementation perspective. The two can be in harmony and allow companies to stay on—and often reduce—budget while being environmentally conscious; being Green becomes a welcome by-product of saving money.[7] This is shown in Figure 1.4, where the balance of cost

Figure 1.4   Costs versus Green Initiatives

savings and Green initiatives is a win-win for organizations, their consumers, and the environment.

Let's bring into the discussion the concepts of investment
versus immediate return. For those who seek to implement Green
initiatives for a quick win and immediate return rather than
longer-term benefits to the organization, Green consumers, and
the environmental challenges we are confronting, this will offset
three key benefits of the Green initiative movement; Green consumerism satisfaction, new Green services and products, and environmental
sustainability. The first is the Green consumer view: Organizations
that make long-term investments in their Green initiatives to be
complementary and in alignment with their needs assist in the
global effort to save the environment and are rewarded with profits over time. Green consumers are weary of organizations being
concerned only with the bottom line quarter after quarter; they
view such behavior as irresponsible for the environmental challenges we are confronted with today. More of the same is not going
to resolve the environmental challenges we all face. Also, the
Green consumer views Green initiatives as a benefit when they are
in alignment with the mission to create environmental sustainability. Steve Johnson, administrator of the U.S. EPA states, "We have
a responsibility to sustain—if not enhance—our natural environment and our nation's economy for future generations."[8] The path
to environmental sustainability is not just short-term cost reductions for organizations but partnerships among the Green economy, Green consumers, and the environment that will sustain
and encourage long-term environmental benefits and economic
growth.

Mutual cost reductions are a win-win for organizations and the
Green consumer and, most important, for the effort in achieving
environmental sustainability, reducing energy consumption, and
reducing carbon footprints. With the main emphasis being on environmental sustainability rather then cost reductions, organizations that
follow this strategy will be viewed by consumers as being a more
socially responsible organization. It is not to say that cost reductions
cannot be achieved with Green initiatives; quite the contrary. Cost
reductions are crucial to the success of Green initiatives. What is
seen as the holy grail of cost reductions is the concept of *mutual*
cost reductions. Green initiatives that mutually offer the organization and its Green consumers cost reductions are very attractive to

both parties. When your consumers can save money and feel they are supporting environmental sustainability, it is good for those who seek and do business with them. Let's consider an example with appliances, say a dishwasher. Offering a dishwasher that has been manufactured via a Green process that has incorporated newer technologies and processes that have reduced manufacturing and operational costs is a win for the organization. Additionally, the dishwasher has achieved ENERGY STAR compliance as an energy-efficient and environmental-friendly unit. Green consumers may win by having these cost savings passed onto them in the price of the dishwasher; more important, the dishwasher operates much more efficiently by using less water and electricity. Thus, the dishwasher helps Green consumers meet their goal of assisting with environmental sustainability.

If your Green initiatives are geared solely to reducing your internal costs and reducing pricing on non-Green related products and services versus offering new or better Green products and/or services, Green consumers may view your behavior as nonbeneficial. Remember, Green consumers are not selfish; they are not looking for cost reductions in products/services that are not environmentally friendly just to save themselves a few dollars. Offering price reductions to a Green consumer's electric power bill where the power is generated from coal-burning power plants is not an attractive offering. Rather, offer to the Green consumer cost-beneficial Green products and services that are part of the organization's overall environmental sustainability goal. The formula for a win-win offering is:

Organization and Green Consumer Cost Reductions +
Green Products/Services + Assisting Environmental
Sustainability = Win-Win

Competitive Forces

Green initiatives are being implemented across the globe, many of them by your competitors. As with many business initiatives that relate to products and/or services, it can be beneficial to those who stay ahead of their competitors to get to the market first. For those in the public sector, speed of delivering products and/or services that are environment-friendly applies as well.

Let's look at first to the market with a public sector example of the United States Postal Service. Its Eco-Friendly Products & Services Web site states:

> The Postal Service is the first mailing or shipping company to achieve Cradle to Cradle[SM] certification for their recyclable packaging. This is environmental "big picture" certification. It starts at the design stage, considers energy and water use through manufacturing, and ends with a product that can be safely recycled. Cradle to Cradle certification comes from McDonough Braungart Design Chemistry. . . . What does this mean for the Postal Service? A half billion Priority Mail and Express Mail packages and envelopes now meet higher environmental standards as more than 15,000 metric tons of carbon equivalent emissions are prevented each year. What does it mean for customers? You can send "greener" packages across the country or around the world—it won't cost you any more.[9]

Green consumers are demanding that organizations implement Green initiatives with speed, productivity, and effectiveness that will offer a higher level of eco-friendly products and services. With the urgency of establishing environmental sustainability much sooner rather than later, speed to market is essential to establish and maintain satisfied Green consumers. Climate change is having a direct impact on global markets, and Achim Steiner, United Nations Environment Programme Executive Director, states:

> Climate change is shaping global markets and global consumer attitudes. There will be winners and losers. Companies who seize the opportunities, who adopt environmental, social and governance policies and who evolve, innovate and respond to these challenges are likely to be the pioneers and industry leaders of the 21st century.[10]

We can relate this need for speed to that of a general in the battlefield. Sun Tzu, in his writings in *The Art of War* two millennia ago, states: "In directing such an enormous army, a speedy victory is the main object and if the war is long delayed, the men's weapon will be blunted."[11] This can be translated to our time with Green initiatives: Organizations that delay in their implementation of Green initiatives will have their efforts blunted with negative market reception and will be in the shadows of those who beat them to market.

For government organizations, speed in implementing Green initiatives can offer a boost in Green job creation, high-tech development, new agriculture products, and much more for citizens and the economy. In times when economies are experiencing job reductions and mass layoffs, it is essential to quickly create jobs and stimulate economies.

Government Regulations and Programs

The impact that is being felt and projected with respect to global warming, reduction in the supply of key economic minerals and resources, and increase in the number of severe storms that affect property and economies has gotten the attention of national governments and the United Nations. These groups have banded together to create and enact programs, regulations, and goals that will strive for environmental sustainability not only within the borders of a single nation but across the globe.

The effects of environmental challenges are not only a private sector challenge that effects profitability and competiveness; due to the severity of repercussions felt by national and global economies and affecting the ability of nation-states to provide for the safety and welfare of their citizens, national governments have recognized these challenges as national and homeland security concerns.

National and Homeland Security   How can the environment impact the security of a nation? The prosperity of a nation relates to economic security; a government's role is to provide an environment where the economy offers organizations and individuals the ability to sustain a stable income or other key resources to support a standard of living now and in the foreseeable future. What affects the economic security of a nation affects its national security. Such economic threats include lower tax revenues for key governmental programs, a reduction in the competiveness of the nation's organizations and citizens in respect to global competition, and the inability to acquire key natural resources.

Looking at one such example, on September 17, 2009, the Obama administration released the Interagency Ocean Policy Task

Force Interim Report, which provided proposals for a comprehensive national approach to uphold our stewardship responsibilities and ensure accountability for our actions. "A National Policy: The Interim Report" proposes a new national policy that recognizes that America's stewardship of the ocean, our coasts, and the Great Lakes is intrinsically and intimately linked to environmental sustainability, human health and well-being, national prosperity, adaptation to climate and other environmental change, social justice, foreign policy, and national and homeland security.[12]

Because the United Nations and the law- and policy-making components of governments have elevated the concern of the impact of the environmental challenges the world is facing this century, government interests and participation in UN Climate Conventions, International Emissions Trading (IET), etc. have increased, as have government-sponsored Green-related programs.

United Nations The term "global warming" puts emphasis on global effects and the need for a global resolution. This is where the United Nations can be of benefit. In 1992 in Rio de Janeiro, the UN Conference on Environment and Development, also known as Earth Summit, convened to create a global treaty that would strive to stabilize greenhouse gases that were contributing to global warming to agree on Greenhouse gas levels that would be effective in obtaining long-term environmental, economic, and social benefits. This international treaty was to be the UN Framework Convention on Climate Change. This treaty needed further modifications and negotiations in order to be ratified by more nation-states; thus, in 1997 in Kyoto, Japan, the Kyoto Protocol was adopted. This protocol requires nation-states between the years of 2008 and 2012 to reduce emissions levels to those of 1990.

The Kyoto Protocol offers incentive and enforcement components to stimulate Green investment. The financial incentives to assist nations in meeting the agreed-on targets in a competitive and cost-effective manner with minimal impact on economies and budgets include:

- **Emissions trading**. Known as the carbon market, that is, European Union Emissions Trading Scheme
- **Clean Development Mechanism (CDM)**. Allows for implementation of an emission-reduction project in developing countries.

Such projects can earn salable certified emission reduction credits, each equivalent to one ton of carbon dioxide, which can be counted toward meeting Kyoto targets.

- **Monitoring and reporting**. Registry, international tracking log.

To date, 184 parties of the convention have ratified the Kyoto Protocol; some exceptions are the United States, India, and China. The United States, although a signatory to the Kyoto Protocol, has neither ratified nor withdrawn from the Protocol, and India and China were given a pass until 2012. With the United States responsible for about 25% of the global warming–related emissions and India and China representing two of the world's fastest-growing polluters, there is much concern regarding how effective the Kyoto Protocol will be in seriously impacting the rise in global temperatures projected for this century. But because India and China are considered developing countries, with other serious problems to overcome, they have been given a pass on the first Kyoto round and do not have to begin making emissions cuts until after 2012. This did not excuse the United States from reducing its greenhouse gas emissions. Thus, the United States has passed the American Recovery and Reinvestment Act and has, through the Department of Energy and the EPA, implemented Climate Change regulations and standards: light-duty vehicle greenhouse gas emissions standards, Corporate Average Fuel Economy Standards, Mandatory Reporting of Greenhouse Gases Rule, and much more. The United States is sending a message regarding the importance of change. As President Obama states:

> So we have a choice to make. We can remain one of the world's leading importers of foreign oil, or we can make the investments that would allow us to become the world's leading exporter of renewable energy. We can let climate change continue to go unchecked, or we can help stop it. We can let the jobs of tomorrow be created abroad, or we can create those jobs right here in America and lay the foundation for lasting prosperity.[13]

Understanding that nation-state leaders would have to deal with private and public sector organizations to implement, audit, report, and meet the principles of the Kyoto Protocol, the United Nations has provided a statement for business leaders to show their

"CARING FOR CLIMATE: THE BUSINESS LEADERSHIP PLATFORM"

A Statement by the Business Leaders of the UN Global Compact

WE, THE BUSINESS LEADERS OF THE UN GLOBAL COMPACT:

RECOGNIZE THAT:
1. Climate Change is an issue requiring urgent and extensive action on the part of governments, business and citizens if the risk of serious damage to global prosperity and security is to be avoided.
2. Climate change poses both risks and opportunities to all parts of the business sector, everywhere. It is in the interest of the business community, as well as responsible behavior, for companies and their associations to play a full part in increasing energy efficiency and reducing carbon emissions to the atmosphere and, where possible, assisting society to respond to those changes in the climate to which we are already committed.

COMMIT TO:
1. Taking practical actions now to increase the efficiency of energy usage and to reduce the carbon burden of our products, services and processes, to set voluntary targets for doing so, and to report publicly on the achievement of those targets annually in our Communication on Progress.
2. Building significant capacity within our organizations to understand fully the implications of climate change for our business and to develop a coherent business strategy for minimizing risks and identifying opportunities.
3. Engaging fully and positively with our own national governments, inter-governmental organizations and civil society organizations to develop policies and measures that will provide an enabling framework for the business sector to contribute effectively to building a low carbon economy.
4. Working collaboratively with other enterprises nationally and sectorally, and along our value-chains, by setting standards and taking joint initiatives aimed at reducing climate risks, assisting with adaptation to climate change and enhancing climate-related opportunities.
5. Becoming an active business champion for rapid and extensive response to climate change with our peers, employees, customers, investors and the broader public.

EXPECT FROM GOVERNMENTS:
1. The urgent creation, in close consultation with the business community and civil society, of comprehensive, long-term and effective legislative and fiscal frameworks designed to make markets work for the climate, in particular policies and mechanisms intended to create a stable price for carbon;
2. Recognition that building effective public-private partnerships to respond to the climate challenge will require major public investments to catalyze and support business and civil society led initiatives, especially in relation to research, development, deployment and transfer of low carbon energy technologies and practices.
3. Vigorous international cooperation aimed at providing a robust global policy framework within which private investments in building a low carbon economy can be made, as well as providing financial and other support to assist those countries that require help to realize their own climate mitigation and adaptation targets whilst achieving poverty alleviation, energy security and natural resource management.

AND WILL:
1. Work collaboratively on joint initiatives between public and private sectors and through them achieve a comprehensive understanding of how both public and private sectors can best play a pro-active and leading role in meeting the climate challenge in an effective way.
2. Invite the UN Global Compact to promote the public disclosure of actions taken by the signatories to this Statement and, in cooperation with UNEP and the WBCSD, communicate on this on a regular basis, starting July 2008.

Figure 1.5   Caring for Climate: The Business Leadership Platform
Source: United Nations Global Compact. "Caring for Climate: The Business Leadership Platform," July 2007.

endorsement of the effort of caring for the climate under the UN Global Compact (see Figure 1.5). Endorsement of the statement allows organizations to demonstrate executive leadership and make organizational changes in favor of implementing more strategic and effective Green initiative that are directed toward Green consumers, investors, and government regulators.

Beyond Kyoto and Post-2012 The UN utilizes two tools in its global warming efforts: the convention and a treaty. The convention is the mechanism and forum for UN members to meet and encourage greenhouse reductions and targets. To make the targets binding and enforceable, a ratified treaty is required. This is an ongoing process, because treaties expire and may require replacements.

The UN was prepared and hopeful for a new treaty to be agreed on when the Kyoto Protocol expired. Thus, a convention (COP15) took place in Copenhagen, Denmark, in December 2009. Yvo de Boer, executive secretary of the United Nations Framework Convention on Climate Change (UNFCCC), in an interview with Environment & Energy Publishing, mentioned the four essentials points needing resolution that could assist in the calling for an international agreement in Copenhagen:[14]

1. How much are the industrialized countries willing to reduce their greenhouse gas emissions?
2. How much are major developing countries, such as China and India, willing to do to limit emissions growth?
3. How is the help needed by developing countries to engage in reducing their emissions and adapting to the impacts of climate change going to be financed?
4. How is that money going to be managed?

The result of the conference was an accord that had no legal binding. Thus, a ratified treaty to succeed the Kyoto Protocol did not occur. The UNFCCC will host additional COPs; a schedule is posted on its Web site at: http://unfccc.int/meetings/unfccc_calendar/items/2655.php.

Government Programs Across the globe, national and local governments are implementing Green-related programs to encourage, sustain, and create additional Green initiatives for their citizens and businesses. Many of these programs are due to Kyoto Protocol compliance, governmental regulation, and/or Green consumer demands. They come in the form of loans, subsidies, tax credits, partnerships, and the like. A few of the many types of programs that have been created and implemented are listed next, by country.

- **United States**. The EPA has created a government-backed program titled ENERGY STAR that allows businesses and individuals a way to help reduce energy use by utilizing superior energy efficiency products (i.e., appliances, air-conditioners, etc.) The program keeps expanding to certify additional product lines. Additionally, the Green Power Partnership works with a wide variety of leading organizations—from Fortune 500 companies to local, state, and federal governments, and a growing number of colleges and universities. Top Partner Rankings highlight the annual Green Power purchases of leading organizations in the United States and across individual industry sectors; the rankings can be viewed at: www.epa.gov/greenpower/toplists/partner100.htm. These Green Power purchases help reduce the environmental impacts of electricity use and support the development of new renewable generation capacity nationwide. Purchase amounts reflect U.S. operations only and are sourced from U.S.-based Green Power resources. Organizations can meet EPA purchase requirements using any combination of three different product options: (1) Renewable Energy Certificates, (2) on-site generation, and (3) utility Green Power products.
- **Australia**. Green Loans is a new Australian government initiative to help Australians tackle climate change. The Green Loans program will assist Australian families in installing solar, water-saving, and energy-efficient products via a free Home Sustainability Assessment and report, along with up to a $10,000 Green Loans subsidy.
- **Brazil**. There is a nationwide program financed by the government to phase out automobile fuels derived from fossil fuels, such as gasoline, in favor of ethanol produced from sugarcane.
- **Canada**. Canada launched a program to offer individual citizens a nonrefundable tax credit to help cover the cost of public transit.
- **United Kingdom**. The government is putting £100 million (US$175 million) into a new £200 million investment program, jointly funded by government and business, to speed up the introduction of new low-carbon vehicles onto Britain's roads.

Visit your local and national government Web sites or offices to learn about programs being implemented and new ones that are in the planning stages. Your organization could benefit substantially from one of these programs. In addition, you can become active in offering feedback and comments to assist with new programs. Other avenues could include the use of Green consultants and lobbyists to assist you with your Green initiative needs.

Green Consumer Demands

Green consumers are demanding that both public and private organizations offer Green products and/or services. It is here where Green consumers will utilize their pocketbook, ethics, and drive in making a personal impact on saving the planet. Green consumers are not entirely new consumers; there has been a level of Green consumer demands on organizations in the past (i.e., organic food offerings, solar and wind power, mass-transit systems, etc.). There are also many names for Green consumers, including ethical consumers, Earth-Friendly Buyers, eco-friendly shoppers, and organic consumers.

Green Consumer Demand Example

A CNNMoney.com article offers insight into Green consumer demands during an interview with the Dell chief executive. According to the article, Michael Dell and his company will now recycle your computer hardware for free—even if you're not buying anything new from Dell. What turned the company around? "Michael Dell cites several factors—consumer demand, the threat of regulation and the recognition that electronic waste, or e-waste, is a significant problem."

Source: M. Gunther, "Dell Gets on the Environmental Bandwagon," CNNMoney .com (2007); http://money.cnn.com/2007/03/08/magazines/fortune/pluggedin_ gunther_dellrecycle.fortune/index.htm

With much of the world embarking on efforts to reduce greenhouse gases in an official capacity, organizations now have greater interest in what Green consumers have to say. But will this delay in truly listening to Green consumers be fatal to global efforts? How much will those organizations just starting Green initiatives have to do to play catch up? Some would say it is never too late to start; others are saying it is too little too late. Nevertheless, we will focus on an optimistic and competitive approach, which is to listen to the market and these Green consumers to enhance competiveness, increase the value of your products and/or services, and strive to contribute to the goal of reducing our global environmental impact that is going to be center stage for the remainder of this century.

What are the demands of the Green consumers? Are they substantially different from that of other consumers, and do they require substantial marketing shifts? Green consumer demands vary somewhat, due to the specifics of the Green products and/or services they are consuming. As mentioned earlier, Green consumers are not entirely new consumers; they are consumers who are asking for the same level of customer satisfaction with the purchase of Green-related products versus non-Green products. A shift has occurred due to the recent focus on the need to reduce greenhouse gases and establish environmentally sustainable process and polices. An example would be that non-Green consumers demand very low electricity kilowatt fees, while Green consumers demand that electric power creation be made from larger percentages of Green power (wind, solar, hydroelectric, etc.) versus coal-generated power. The demands made by Green consumers are not based solely on cost savings; they seek to have a direct effect on the global environmental challenge. I myself have experienced this shift by changing my electric plan to having a percentage of wind power generation, despite being charged a little more per kilowatt per hour versus a 100% non-Green electric plan.

With so much at stake to reduce greenhouse gas (GHG) emissions, Green consumers are taking this opportunity to make their demands heard and become actionable. Thus, Green consumers are less tolerant of those organizations that are not offering Green products and/or services or attempting to reduce their carbon footprint. A win-win example is auto manufacturing, where the manufacturing plant for a gasoline-alternative car (electric, biofuels, etc.) is built with Green building processes that emit very few greenhouse gases. Consumers benefit from reducing their carbon footprint by replacing a gasoline-guzzling automobile.

A list of demands relevant to Green consumers to satisfy their needs and eco-conscious consumption requirements is presented next.

- **Green consumers are passionate and want Green businesses to be as well**. No Greenwashing tactics will be tolerated. Sell by example. Promote your organization's Green initiatives to make Green consumers aware of your efforts, sincerity, and socially responsible actions. Participate in surveys by leading magazines, research organizations, and government programs so your organization can be listed when it reaches certain criteria, performance levels, and customer satisfaction levels.

- **Organizations need to have Green compliance validation**. Green consumers will ask for some type of certification and validation of your products/services as being Green. One such practice is "ecolabeling" which is a voluntary method of environmental performance certification practiced around the world, via the use of an ecolabel. The label identifies overall environmental preference of a product or service within a specific product/service category based on life cycle considerations.[15] Types of programs include U.S. EPA ENERGY STAR, Green Seal Program, Global Ecolabeling Network, European Union Ecolabel Award Scheme, and Canadian EcoLog TM Program. Your organization should seek Green certification to validate and certify your Green initiatives.

- **Green consumers want to participate and feel involved**. Consumers who are involved feel empowered and gain more value from what they are purchasing. Green consumers are no different. Having facilities that gather feedback and ideas for new products and/or services from Green consumers can be a win-win for an organization. Green consumers like to participate in surveys and joint research efforts. Having product demonstrations in local communities, TV talk shows, trade shows, and other venues that offer consumers the ability to comment, critique, and evaluate your products before purchasing them can be of benefit to an organization.

- **Green consumers want organizations to be transparent**. Green consumers shop smart and ethically. Shopping smart means knowing what's behind the label,[16] and Green consumers review buyers' guides, organizational Web sites, and other information sources. Hiding information and not being forthcoming in your Green initiatives will not be effective in attracting and sustaining Green consumers.

- **Green consumers want organizations that act genuinely**.
  Organizations embarking on Green initiatives need to show
  sincerity, determination, and a will to sustain these efforts over
  the long haul. Organizations viewing Green demands as fads
  and short term will have challenges with Green consumers.
  Green consumers are not expecting that organizations be fault-
  less in their Green initiative efforts but do expect a genuine
  commitment.

It is up to your organization to determine if it views the Green
consumer movement as one that is marketable and profitable. Is it a
group of consumers who are part of a fad, or is it one that is sustainable for a longer term that can justify the expenditures and time
in making Greener products/or service? For those who are mandated by market pressure, regulations, etc., in dealing with Green
consumers, you will have to evaluate their demands and take up
the task of aligning your products and/or services to satisfy them.
It is highly recommended that your organization perform effective Green market research looking at all of the drivers that relate
to Green initiatives to help you obtain a more holistic view of the
potential benefits in dealing with Green consumers.

Green consumer demands should be understood and respected
by those who have interest in marketing and selling to them. But this
effort must offer some level of strategic benefit for an organization. One
such strategic benefit is to increase the level of customer satisfaction being reported. Figure 1.6 graphically depicts that Green consumer demands when offered with productive customer satisfaction
processes can result in satisfied Green consumers, which should yield
strategic benefits to your organization. Customer satisfaction is the
number-one key performance indicator (KPI) that many organizations monitor and strive to achieve; here the benefits of catering to
Green consumers has high potential for the organization as a whole.

All of these Green consumer demands are with benefit to an
organization and the effort extended to the Green consumer by the organization's customer service and marketing processes. Some key factors that can offer win-win scenarios for an organization to strategically
benefit from by understanding Green consumers are listed next.

- **Green consumers are not fad or trend buyers**. They are not
  short-term buyers whom you will not see when another fad

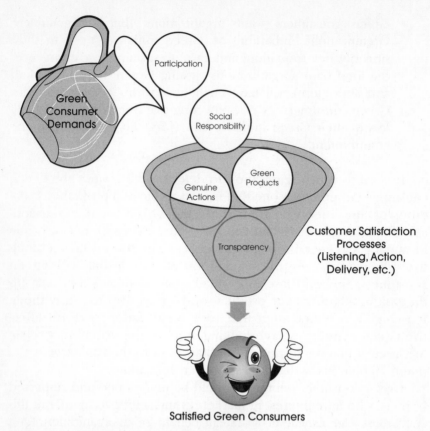

Satisfied Green Consumers

Figure 1.6   Green Consumer Satisfaction

becomes hot. Green consumers have a deep and concerning
passion with their mission of being responsible consumers
and consider this responsibility a lifetime commitment.

- **Green consumers are active buyers.** "Build it and they will
come" has some relevance with Green consumers, who are
constantly looking for products and/or services that offer
verified, certified, and substantial assistance with the environmental challenges of this century.
- **Green consumers may pay more for Green products and/
or services.** This is not to say that Green consumers are not
interested in a good deal that will offer a lower price for a comparable product that is not as Green. Offering cost reductions

(thus, price is one component of this) along with your Green products and/or services is more enticing than offering price and cost increases to Green consumers. Nevertheless, if warranted, Green consumers will see a slight markup in price as acceptable if it helps them with their eco-conscious goals. Green consumers will allow organizations to satisfy their demands at a slight additional premium, so organizations can view the business relationship with these consumers as having some flexibility. Don't let the drive to market and sell to Green consumers be based solely on the idea of possible price markups, for Green consumers will see straight through your shallow efforts. Effective and productive products and/or services with a respectable price tag will be more beneficial to your dealings with Green consumers.

- **Green consumers buy across many product lines**. The market for Green consumers is vast, for they are looking for products for their home, transportation, recreational, and personal needs. The products can range from energy-efficient appliances, eco-friendly cleaning chemicals, solar panels for the home, to electric or hybrid cars.

Benefits of Green Initiatives with IT Overview

The previous sections of this chapter have given insight into the driving forces that will encourage organizations to implement Green initiatives. These Green initiatives will require the participation, collaboration, and cohesiveness of many of the organization's resources to achieve maximum benefits to the organization, Green consumers, and the environment. One such organizational resource is the IT department. The IT departmental components that can benefit an organization's strategic Green initiatives include:

- Human resources
- Technology
- Offerings
- IT-business relationship

Green initiative efforts with the IT department build on the strategic IT-business relationship that already should exist within organizations. This relationship has a mission to strategically enhance an organization's profitability, productivity, efficiency, competitiveness, and compliance, and to positively affect many other strategic goals. The IT department brings to the relationship resources and knowledge; thus, IT can assist an organization with its Green initiatives. Furthermore, with many Green initiatives requiring computer and network technology as well as application software and Web sites, it is the IT department that can satisfy these requirements through its resources and offerings.

It is the strength and the level of alignment of the IT-business relationship that is essential for the success of Green initiatives. Additionally, the IT department has human and technical resources along with products that can be utilized to complement the organization's strategic Green initiatives. So, let's review this special IT-business relationship. Chapter 2 builds on this section and goes into much more detail.

Human Resources

The human resources within an IT department can vary vastly, depending on the size of the organization, funding, organization structure, and much more. Nevertheless, some key resources available to the organization in assisting with its Green initiatives include:

- Chief information officer (CIO)
- Green IT advisors
- Directors and managers
- IT architects
- System architects
- Data center engineers
- Database administrators
- Network engineers
- System analysts
- Help desk/support

Additionally, in global organizations, IT resources may be dispersed worldwide. When implementing global Green initiatives, these global IT resources have knowledge not only of their IT responsibilities but of the local community and much more. Furthermore, global employees who are also Green consumers can offer you valuable input and feedback on your Green initiatives; thus, it is highly recommended to call on these global resources.

Technology

As with human resources, the types of technology utilized within an IT department can vary substantially. Nevertheless, some key areas of technology applicable to most organizations in assisting with its Green initiatives are listed next.

- Data centers: power, cooling, hosting, virtualization
- Networks: intranet, Internet, extranet, mobile, wireless, wired
- Desktops/laptops
- Servers: file, print, application, web, database, management
- Disk storage: storage area network (SAN), network attached storage (NAS), virtual storage, portable storage
- Mobile devices: PDAs, cell phones
- Backup/restore: tape units, disk systems, appliances
- Software development tools: Web applications, Win form thick clients, etc.
- Videoconferencing and teleconferencing systems

These technologies all offer eco-friendly options and features that can complement an organization's Green initiative efforts. It could be as simple as utilizing power-saving features with desktop computers and laptops to using server virtualization technology to reduce the number of servers in the data center, thus possibly reducing the organization's energy consumption costs. Furthermore, the use of videoconferencing technology can help an organization reduce travel that contributes to the emission of greenhouse gases. These are just a few of the benefits of engaging IT to assist with the organization's strategic Green initiatives.

IT Offerings

Beyond the human resources and technology of an IT department are what is considered its offerings: skill sets, capabilities, and functionality that the department offers the organization to assist with business challenges and needs. IT offerings work with strategic information systems that are aligned to assist with the organization's strategic objectives. It is not that strategic information systems are essentially different applications; their impact on the business due to the changes they enable or cause is different.[17]

These offerings are defined in a way that the business can relate to and map to its needs, thus removing much of techie terms and IT jargon. Some examples of offerings that can be mapped to Green initiatives include:

- Green IT assessment, procurement, and advising
- Asset management
- Application portfolio management
- Application development
- IT-business application architecture and planning
- IT systems and data center architecture and management
- Enterprise data management/master data management
- Tactical, operational, and strategic reporting
- Business intelligence analytics and predictive analysis
- Knowledge management
- Collaboration and content management
- Business performance management
- Auditing and regulatory compliance
- Video-conferencing and communication
- Project management

How can the IT department help with reducing nondirect IT-related energy consumption? It can do so via its offerings. The managing, analysis, and control of Green initiatives can be done through the application development IT offering of tactical, operational, and strategic reporting and/or business intelligence analytics and predictive analysis. The offerings can allow an organization to measure, track, and report the Green initiative objectives, goals, project statuses and costs, and environmental and economic KPIs that will assist in determining what type of action should be taken and making necessary adjustments to Green initiative strategies. These assessments can be done via a Balanced Scorecard application, ad hoc reporting tools, custom report development, dashboard deployments, and much more. Chapter 2 goes into more detail on these offerings.

In one type of Green initiative common in organizations that are striving to reduce their overall energy usage and costs, the IT department assists via its own internal operations (data center, server, desktop and laptop power consumption) as well as with offerings to reduce energy costs that are not directly IT related (i.e., office lighting, corporate vehicle fleet, etc.) An organization's IT department may have experience in Green initiatives before the overall organization engages in environmentally sustainable practices. The reason is that the IT department is constantly striving to reduce its energy and power usage as well as its overall operational costs.

The IT department engaged in the assessment and procurement of Green IT equipment (i.e., ENERGY STAR) can advise regarding the organization's overall energy efficiency goals. Even if the equipment is not IT related, involve your IT department in your efforts to procure energy-efficient equipment by listening to their experiences, challenges, and vendor discussions. Their experiences could be used as a model for the rest of the organization.

IT-Business Relationship

Strategic organizational goals should view Green initiatives as essential and of value, not as being nonproductive overhead costs, efforts that reduce competiveness and profitability. With driving forces outside the organization demanding and requiring that it produce Greener products and services and reduce its operational carbon footprint, Green initiatives should become part of an organization's strategic goals. IT offerings should be incorporated through the strategic IT-business relationship. Let's look at one such Green initiative effort, reducing energy usage, where the IT-business relationship can be of substantial value. Various parts of an organization have common energy consumption needs. The IT data center is a significant energy consumer, as is manufacturing and heavy industrial operations. Through joint effort, IT and the business can work to reduce power consumption of computer systems within the data center, throughout the manufacturing area, and throughout the organization, along with the energy consumption of power systems in both areas.

Business analysts from the business units working side by side with IT personnel in many strategic IT-business projects can help create the bridge between the two entities. Additionally, IT workshops offered to business personnel help educate and inform them about IT capabilities and offerings. It is this collaboration, cohesiveness, and synergy between IT and the business that can lead to productive and effective Green initiative solutions and implementations.

CIO: Executive-Level Leadership For Green initiatives to have strategic benefits and leadership, executives of the organization must support Green initiatives. The CIO is one such executive-level role that is of significant importance to the success of an organization's Green initiatives. The CIO oversees the human resources, technology, and offerings of the IT department. The CIO can assist with Green initiatives from within his or her own department and through the overall IT offerings. Having CIOs who are acting in a Green manner is also a plus for the organization's Green efforts. CIOs who take responsibility for having their IT departments become Greener will help the organization in its Green efforts.

According to exclusive research, CIOs are beginning to think Green. Stricter government regulations, rising energy costs, and the growing awareness that sustainability is a real business concern are pushing companies to strategize how they will meet future energy demands and calls for carbon emissions data. Green IT is making inroads in the data center; CIOs are also starting to realize that it is only the beginning. Fifty-four percent of IT leaders responding to a *CIO* magazine survey about Green IT report that their organizations have environmental sustainability goals for information technology. In other words, they are trying to reduce IT's impact on the planet.[18]

Cross-Functional Exposure and Experience IT department human resources, technology, and offerings serve the company as a whole, thus crossing business functionality lines and working with various departments on a daily basis. Thus, IT human resources often are part of a cross-functional team that includes persons from many different functional business areas and levels of expertise. It is this type of business exposure that increases the business knowledge of IT personnel and their ability to be part of projects that aim to solve business goals and needs. IT personnel benefit from crossing the functional business lines of an organization via exposure, participation, and making business contacts, thus increasing their value as participants in the organization's strategic Green initiatives.

SWOT Analysis of IT-Business Relationship A tool that can be used to analyze an organization's IT-Business relationship with respect to Green initiatives is called the strengths, weaknesses, opportunities, and threat (SWOT) analysis. Figure 1.7 offers a graphical example of a SWOT analysis.

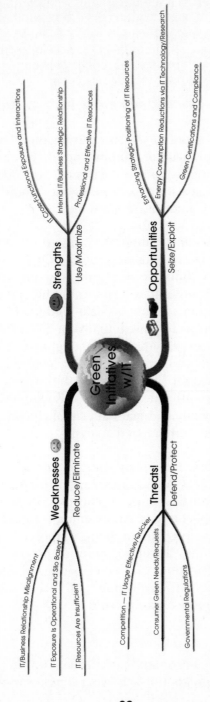

Figure 1.7 SWOT Analysis: Green Initiatives with IT Department

SWOT Analysis

A strategic planning method used to evaluate the **s**trengths, **w**eaknesses, **o**pportunities, and **t**hreats that assists in defining possible favorable and unfavorable consequences of internal and external factors to a business activity, venture, or process.

SWOT analysis is a tool for auditing an organization and its environment. It is the first stage of planning and helps marketers focus on key issues. Strengths and weaknesses are internal factors. Opportunities and threats are external factors. Some guidelines to follow for your SWOT analysis are listed next.

- Be honest and realistic about the strengths and weaknesses of your organization's IT-business relationship.
- SWOT analysis should distinguish between where the relationship is currently and where it could be in the future.
- Utilize input from executives, stakeholders, IT, business analysts, and others as to ensure that your SWOT analysis is specific and removes gray areas and ambiguity.
- SWOT is meant to better your IT-business relationship in a way to make it more beneficial to the overall organization. Competitors are utilizing SWOT in this manner as well.
- Remove complexity and maintain simplicity but be thorough.
- Offer a detailed, summarized analysis.

Complete a SWOT analysis of your organization's IT-business relationship. Verify that weaknesses can be reduced and eliminated by strengths and that those threats can be protected against and converted to opportunities. An example is to defend from the threat of government regulations being imposed on the organization by turning it into an opportunity to be compliant and to establish Green certifications and eco-labeling, which offer Green consumers much-needed verification and justification in doing business with eco-friendly organizations.

Summary

Green initiatives are becoming mainstream within organizations that have the strategic goal of achieving long-term environmental sustainability. With demand from consumers, competition, regulatory compliance, and the need for organizations to reduce energy consumption, reduce their carbon footprint, and show a higher level of social responsibility and less Greenwashing, Green initiatives are becoming a necessity. Organizations can achieve great benefits from the implementation of Green initiatives, especially when utilizing the IT department's resources and offerings in an integrated, cohesive, and collaborative manner.

The IT department has a vast amount of resources and offerings that can be used to complement and assist Green initiatives (i.e., technical and human resources, application development and hosting offerings, and much more). Additionally, when the IT department supports and equips many of the organization's business units and functions, the IT-business relationship can be a benefit. The executive level of the IT department—the CIO—can also be a key participant, planner, and partner within the organization's executive leadership.

Notes

1. A. Gore, *Our Choice: A Plan to Solve the Climate Crisis* (New York: Melcher Media, 2009).
2. Sources: Annual Energy Outlook (DOE/EIA-0383[2007]); International Energy Outlook 2007 (DOE/EIA-0484[2007]); Inventory of U.S. Greenhouse Gas Emissions and Sinks: 1990–2005 (EPA 430-R-07-002 [April 2007]).
3. A. Marker, E. Johnsen, and C. Caswell, "Performance Improvement," *International Society of Performance Improvement* 48, no. 8 (2009).
4. O. C. Ferrell, J. Fraedrich, and L. Ferrell, *Business Ethics: Ethical Decision Making and Cases* (Boston: Houghton Mifflin, 2005).
5. Microsoft Environment, "Fostering Alternative Ways to Commute at Microsoft," 2009. Retrieved from Microsoft Web site at: www.microsoft.com/ environment/our_commitment/articles/alternative_commuting.aspx
6. Environmental Defense Fund, "McDonald's—Styrofoam Packaging," 2009; www.edf.org/page.cfm?tagID=56
7. Logicalis, "Experience IT Make It Better," 2008; www.us.logicalis.com/pdf/Green %20IT%20Feature%20Story.pdf
8. United States Environmental Protection Agency, "What Is Sustainability?" 2009; http://yosemite.epa.gov/r10/oi.nsf/b724ca698f6054798825705700693650/ 2da335d4a914342c88256fc400784f91!OpenDocument
9. United States Postal Service. "Eco-friendly Products and Services," 2009; www .usps.com/green/eco.htm
10. United Nations, www.unglobalcompact.org/docs/networks_around_world_ doc/Regional_Meetings/Europe/Presentations_Folder/Climate_Change_ UNEP.pdf

11. G. A. Michelson, *Sun Tzu: The Art of War for Managers; 50 Strategic Rules* (Avon, MA: Adams Media Corporation, 2001).
12. White House, "Council on Environmental Quality," 2009; www.whitehouse.gov/administration/eop/ceq/initiat ives/oceans/
13. White House, "Energy & Environment," 2009; www.whitehou se.gov/issues/energy_and_environment
14. M. Von Bulow, "The Essentials in Copenhagen," United Nations, 2009; http://en.cop15.dk/news/view+news? newsid=876
15. Global Ecolabeling Network, "What Is Ecolabeling?" 2004; http://globalecolabelling.net/whatis.html
16. Ecologist, "Consumerism," 2009; http://theecologist.net-genie.co.uk/take_action/101_Ways_Forward/271314/consumerism.html
17. J. Ward and J. Peppard, *Strategic Planning for Information Systems* (Hoboken, NJ: John Wiley & Sons, 2002).
18. Elina Varon, "The Greening of IT," *CIO*, 2008, www.cio.com/article/196450/The_Greening_of_IT

CHAPTER

2

IT Resources and Offerings to Assist Green Initiatives

G reen initiatives can be served by many organizational resources. One such valuable business entity is the IT department. With so many eco-friendly options applicable to IT department resources, here the IT department's awareness of its own Greening abilities can benefit the organization as a whole. The IT department's resources, both human and technical, along with its experience in working across business functions can greatly benefit productive and effective organizational Green initiative planning and implementation.

This chapter discusses in detail the specific IT resources and offerings—IT research, technology, human resources, and partnerships—that can assist in accomplishing an organization's Green initiatives. It is here that one can visualize much of what is available to Green initiative efforts in one's own IT department.

The human and technical resources within an IT department can be beneficial, experienced, and productive resources in assisting an organization in its Green initiatives. Some of these key resources are:

- Chief Information Officer (CIO)
- Green IT advisors
- Data center architects
- Application developers

Furthermore, the IT department's offerings are derived from its resources and are beneficial to Green initiative efforts as well. IT offerings can be summarized in two categories: general and specific. General IT offerings are typical across many organizations because they are technology related and universal. Examples of such general IT offerings include:

- Previous knowledge and experience in Green initiatives
- Positioned as a strategic partner within organizations
- User and implementer of technology (i.e., network, server, data center, application, etc.)
- Green initiative technology implementers (i.e., video tele-conferencing, server and disk storage virtualization, business applications)

The types of IT department offerings that are more specific to Green initiatives are those that are tailored, customized, and implemented for supporting a specific aspect or the entirety of a Green initiative. Types of specific IT department offerings are:

- Creates dashboards and Balanced Scorecards with Green initiatives' key performance indicators (KPIs) from application developers
- Deployment of a third-party custom application to specifically support Green initiatives (i.e., environmental management system)
- Creates collaborative project and team-site portals for Green initiative efforts
- Data center architecture and management offering to address data center energy consumption reductions and other Greening processes
- Green advising to environmental sustainability steering committee

Understanding that Green initiatives need to be strategically planned and implemented, an organization will reach out to its strengths and resources to assist in the effort. One such valuable resource is the IT department. This relationship can be shown by the next formula.

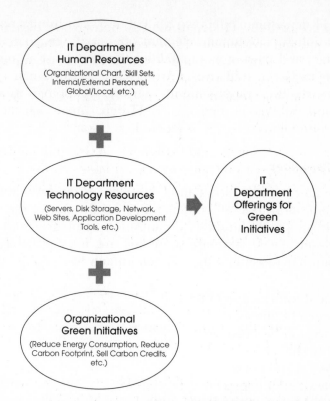

Figure 2.1   Components of IT Department Offerings for Green Initiatives

IT Department Human Resources + IT Department
Technology Resources + Organizational Green Initiatives
= IT Department Offerings for Green Initiatives

In addition, Figure 2.1 shows that IT department offerings for Green initiatives are a summation of the resources of the IT department and business alignment.

IT Resources

Green initiatives will require the participation, collaboration, and cohesiveness of many of the organization's resources to achieve the maximum benefits to the organization, Green consumers, and the environment. One such beneficial organizational component is the information technology (IT) department.

The IT department offers two types of resources: human resources and technology. The human element offers skill sets, experiences, knowledge, and passion as capabilities that can assist an organization with its Green initiatives. Furthermore, because many Green initiatives require computer and network technology as well as application and Web hosting, it is the IT department that can satisfy these requirements through its technology resources.

Human Resources

The human resources within an IT department can vary vastly from one organization to another, depending on the size of the organization it supports, funding, organization structure, and much more. Nevertheless, there are some key resources available to the organization in assisting with its Green initiatives:

- Chief Information Officer
- Green IT advisors
- Directors and managers
- IT architects
- System architects
- Data center engineers
- Database administrators
- Network engineers
- System analysts
- Application developers
- Help desk/support

Over and over as I consulted with many Fortune 500 companies, I have noted that human resources are an organization's most vital and important resource, far more important than technology, manufacturing, and others. Thus, it is critical to maximize the efficiency, performance, and utilization of the organization's human resources during Green initiative efforts.

Global Personnel   Additionally, in global organizations, IT resources may be dispersed throughout the globe. Thus, when implementing global Green initiatives, it is these global IT resources who have knowledge not only of their IT responsibilities, but also of the local culture, local Green consumer needs and desires, and much more.

The value systems and norms of a country influence the costs of doing business there; thus, the costs of doing business in a country influence the ability of organizations to establish a competitive advantage in the global marketplace.[1] Utilize global employees to increase the organization's Green initiatives benefits, thus possibly increasing its competitiveness. Global employees who are also Green consumers can offer a global organization valuable input and feedback on Green initiatives. Global employees can be:

- Surveyed to gather insight into specific regional markets
- Utilized as reviewers and/or testers of Green products/services
- Utilized as first Green consumers as an example and to showcase Green products
- Eyes and ears of how nonemployee Green consumers view the organization's Green image and Green products/services across the globe
- Keys to understanding social, political, and cultural specifics that can benefit Green initiatives in the regional and globally

Green Organizational Charts Many organizations that have already embarked on their Green initiative effort have revised their organizational chart with new Green-related management, teams, and personnel. This occurs when Green initiatives have executive leadership and are seen as of strategic importance to the organization. Figure 2.2 shows a sample organizational chart with Green-related references. Although it may seem that changing an organization's culture is difficult, it isn't impossible.[2] The modifications to the organizational chart should continue to enforce an ethical and customer-responsive organization culture.

Green initiatives of an organization are often wrapped up into the topic of environmental sustainability (ES). This is reflected in the organizational chart, where the ES entity directly reports to the CEO of the organization, in part because of the strategic value and importance of ES to the organization, employees, customers, and investors. The strategic practice of ES is not a part-time role for an employee, and should not be treated as an organizational task of minimal importance or as a nuisance to organizational operations. Rather it should be of strategic interest and implementation. Thus, the organizational chart should reflect its significance by its relation to the top executive level and its integration throughout the organization. Depending on the

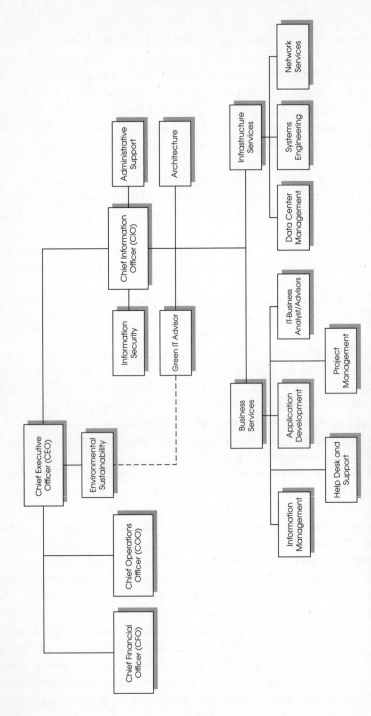

Figure 2.2 Green-Related Organizational Chart—Executive View

size of the organization, the ES entity may be represented by a Chief Sustainability Officer (CSO), Chief Environmental Strategist (CES), vice president of ES, or others. In May 2009, it was reported that SAP, the multinational software giant, announced that it was appointing its first-ever CSO as part of an effort to reduce carbon emissions and save energy. In fact, a number of other big companies, like Sun Microsystems, Georgia Pacific, and DuPont, already have CSOs.[3]

The link between the ES entity and the IT department is shown via the Green IT advisor entity, who is trained and competent in many of the ES practices, offerings, and technologies that an IT department can utilize to become Greener. Additionally, this Green IT advisor is part of the organization's ES virtual team, educating and informing employees on the benefits of utilizing IT resources and offerings with Green initiative efforts.

Figure 2.3 offers a view into a different type of organizational chart that depicts the Green programs and policies of a city. The figure relates the programs and policies to the city departments, which can be seen as different shadings and are mapped to the chart at the bottom right of the figure. Those responsible for each Green-related program are listed. There is no direct mention of the City of Long Beach Technology Services Department (TSD). Is it involved with the city's Green initiatives? The answer is yes! From a strategic perspective, TSD is involved with a wide variety of issues, such as long-term planning for information and communications systems, emergency preparedness and disaster recovery, interoperable communications between public agencies, network and data security, and telecommunications regulatory changes. Moreover, TSD is addressing fundamental shifts in technology used by city departments, including the transition away from mainframe-based information systems, the utilization of environmentally Green hardware, and the implementation of Internet-based voice communications systems. Furthermore, TSD leverages technology, such as the Internet and cable television, to provide the public with access to important city information and services, such as Green programs and policies.[4]

Technology Resources

As with human resources, the types of technology utilized within an IT department can vary substantially. Nevertheless, some key areas

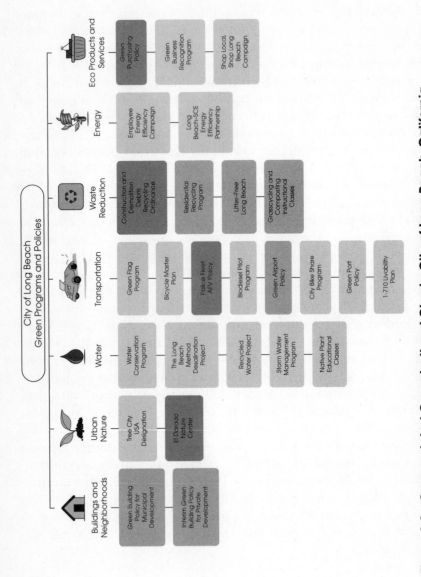

Figure 2.3 Green-related Organizational Chart—City of Long Beach, California

Source: www.longbeach.gov/civica/filebank/blobdload.asp?BlobID=21343

of technology available to most organizations in assisting with its Green initiatives are listed next.

- Data centers: power, cooling, hosting
- Networks: intranet, Internet, extranet, mobile, wireless, wired
- Desktops/laptops
- Servers: file, print, application, database, management, and virtualization
- Disk storage: storage area network (SAN), network attached storage (NAS), and virtualization
- Mobile devices: PDAs, cell phones
- Backup/restore: tape units, disk systems, appliances

These technologies all offer eco-friendly options and features that can complement an organization's Green effort. It could be as simple as utilizing power-saving features with desktop computers and laptops to using server virtualization technology to reduce the number of servers in the data center, thus possibly reducing the organization's energy consumption costs. Furthermore, the use of video-conferencing technology can help an organization reduce travel that contributes to the emission of greenhouse gases. These are just a few of the benefits of engaging IT in assisting with the organization's strategic Green initiatives.

Energy-efficient computing is becoming a priority for businesses and organizations seeking to control costs and reduce their impact on the environment. One way for an organization to reduce power usage is to implement an energy-efficient server infrastructure that facilitates management and allocation of power to computing resources as needed.

As businesses use more servers, and as the servers themselves become more powerful, the amount of electricity it takes to operate them rises proportionately. Faster processors generally draw more power than slower ones and generate more heat, requiring more powerful cooling systems.

The use of videoconferencing technology can assist an organization in reducing travel that contributes to emission of greenhouse gases. Additionally, mobile networks and devices are allowing workers to stay in the field, thus reducing travel back to the corporate office.

There are many benefits of engaging IT to assist with the organization's strategic Green initiatives, so let's dive deeper into some specific IT offerings and their Green-related benefits.

Data Centers   In August 2007 the United States Environmental Protection Agency (EPA) reported to the U.S. Congress on data center energy efficiency:

> During the past five years, increasing demand for computer resources has led to significant growth in the number of data center servers, along with an estimated doubling in the energy used by these servers and the power and cooling infrastructure that supports them. This increase in energy use has a number of important implications, including:
> - increased energy costs for business and government
> - increased emissions, including greenhouse gases, from electricity generation
> - increased strain on the existing power grid to meet the increased electricity demand
> - increased capital costs for expansion of data center capacity and construction of new data centers.
>
> For these reasons, there has been mounting interest in opportunities for energy efficiency in this sector.[5]

Energy Use in Data Centers through 2011   The energy used by an organization and a nation's servers and data centers is significant. Relating this to the United States, it is estimated that this sector consumed about 61 billion kilowatt-hours (kWh) in 2006 (1.5% of total electricity consumption) for a total electricity cost of about $4.5 billion. This estimated level of electricity consumption is more than the electricity consumed by the nation's color televisions and similar to the amount of electricity consumed by approximately 5.8 million average U.S. households (or about 5% of the total housing stock). Federal servers and data centers alone account for approximately 6 billion kWh (10%) of this electricity use, for a total electricity cost of about $450 million annually.

The energy use of the U.S. servers and data centers in 2006 is estimated to be more than double the electricity consumed for this purpose in 2000. One type of server, the volume server, consumed the majority (68%) of electricity consumed by IT equipment in data centers in 2006. The amount of energy used by this type of server more than doubled from 2000 to 2006, which was the largest increase among different types of servers. The power and cooling infrastructure that supports IT equipment in data centers also uses significant energy, accounting for 50% of the total consumption of data centers. Among the different types of data centers, more than one-third (38%) of electricity use is attributable to the nation's largest (i.e., enterprise-class) and most rapidly growing data centers.

Under current efficiency trends, U.S. energy consumption by servers and data centers could nearly double again in another five years (i.e., by 2011) to more than 100 billion kWh, representing a $7.4 billion annual electricity cost. The peak load on the power grid from these servers and data centers is currently estimated to be approximately 7 gigawatts (GW), equivalent to the output of about 15 baseload power plants. If current trends continue, this demand would rise to 12 GW by 2011, which would require an additional 10 power plants.

Figure 2.4 offers insight into the different Green initiative processes that the IT department is involved in to make data centers Greener. Perform an energy use assessment on your organization's data centers. From there you can have an overall look at what types, amount, and

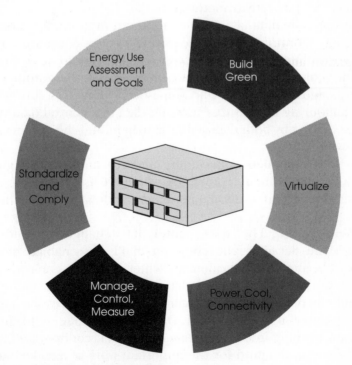

Figure 2.4   Data Center Greening

distribution of energy consumption is occurring, which will give you the information needed to define goals and Green initiatives.

If applicable, organizations that are building new data centers can invoke Green building construction processes (i.e., recycle building materials, solar energy panels on data center roof, etc.). Many organizations that have preexisting data centers can invoke Green building initiatives when expanding or remodeling. The ability to implement virtualization within the data center is a beneficial Green initiative. Reduction in the number of physical servers reduces energy consumption and cooling costs.

This takes us to power, cooling, and connectivity. Data centers are large energy consumers, both to power assets and to cool them. Reduction of energy usage must be a key concern in an organization's effort to become environmentally sustainable and to reduce its carbon footprint. Connectivity is related to networks, data center interconnectivity to remote sites and other globally dispersed data center, and so on. Connectivity consumes energy and has environmental consequences, depending on the type of network infrastructure and the connectivity methods used.

During daily data center operations, an organization would be managing, monitoring, and measuring energy consumption and other environmental performance metrics in order to make changes, redefine goals, and adjust efforts to stay on track with environmentally sustainable goals. This can be accomplished with meters, sensors, and other measuring devices that transmit data to a central data repository for viewing by both data center managers and the organization's executives.

Look to implement data center standards and adhere to government and international regulations, which are listed on Web sites of government and international regulatory bodies and associations.

The Green Grid   The data center has changed considerably through the decades. The evolution of IT has enabled the data center to become the critical nerve center of today's enterprise. The number of data center facilities has increased over time as business demands increase, and each facility houses an increasing amount of more powerful IT equipment. Data center managers around the world are running into limits related to power, cooling, and space, and the rise in demand for the important work of data centers has had a noticeable impact on the world's power grids. The efficiency of data centers has become an important topic of global discussion among end users, policy makers, technology providers, facility architects, and utility companies.

When industry adopts a standard set of measurements, it will be easier for end users to manage their facilities and equipment to achieve optimal energy efficiency. The Green Grid is a global consortium of IT companies and professionals seeking to improve energy efficiency in data centers and business computing ecosystems worldwide. The organization seeks to unite global industry efforts to standardize a common set of metrics, processes, methods, and new technologies to further its common goals.

The Green Grid

A global consortium dedicated to developing and promoting energy efficiency for data centers and business computing ecosystems by:

- Defining meaningful, user-centric models and metrics
- Promoting the adoption of energy efficient standards, processes, measurement methods, and technologies
- Developing standards, measurement methods, processes, and new technologies to improve performance against the defined metrics

Source: www.thegreengrid.org/about-the-green-grid

Join The Green Grid to benefit your organization and industry. Data centers vary considerably—from the age of the facility, to location, to the infrastructure inside it, to the work it produces. By participating in a variety of work groups and user forums, you will be able to add your company's voice to the hundreds of others that are developing the next wave of globally adopted metrics and measurements that will help you achieve data center efficiency.

Desktops/Laptops Power management options are available in desktop/laptop operating systems. One such example is with Microsoft Windows 7 which is designed to conserve energy, provide longer battery life and has enhanced enterprise power manageability. Windows 7 enables IT pros to better manage power and troubleshoot related problems. Similarly, IT pros can centrally control more power management settings on a granular level. These settings include the new options Adaptive Display Brightness, Reserve Battery Notification Level, and Allowing Automatic Sleep with Open Network Files. IT pros can also configure power management settings by using Group Policy preferences.

Managing hundreds, thousands, and hundreds of thousands desktops and laptops within an organization can be a daunting task. To assist with the challenge of ensuring that power savings features are implemented and enabled, there exist desktop management applications, such as Microsoft System Center Configuration Manager 2007 and associated configuration packs. With the Desired Configuration Management pack, organizations can ensure that IT systems comply with ENERGY STAR guidelines. The configuration pack enables organizations to assess display and hibernation settings on Windows XP, Windows Vista, or Windows 7 operating systems.

This configuration pack, whose specifications were developed in partnership with the EPA, enables System Center Configuration Manager 2007 users to assess their client settings against these ENERGY STAR recommendations:

- Have computers enter system standby or hibernate after 30 to 60 minutes of inactivity.
- Have monitors enter sleep mode after 5 to 20 minutes of inactivity.
- Create a warning notification report if screen savers are not disabled. If one is enabled, the wait timeout period should be less than the monitor sleep setting.

Energy Star   ENERGY STAR is a joint program of the EPA and the U.S. Department of Energy that helps save money and protect the environment through energy efficient products and practices. The ENERGY STAR guidelines for computers cover both the hardware devices and the power management features expected of the operating system and applications. The program specifies criteria for hardware manufacturers to achieve defined efficiency levels with recommendations for computer power management settings. Although the ENERGY STAR requirements primarily target hardware manufacturers to specify minimum efficiency ratings, there are also guidelines for computer software. The ENERGY STAR Version 5.0 Specification for Computers was finalized on November 14, 2008.

Desktop and notebook (laptop) computers, game consoles, integrated computer systems, desktop-derived servers, and workstations are all eligible to earn the ENERGY STAR. Those that come with the label are more efficient than ever. When purchasing a new computer, be sure to look for the ENERGY STAR before making your final decision. You should be able to find the label on the products and packaging as well as in product literature and on Web sites. EPA's ENERGY STAR Web site enables users to search for labeled notebooks/laptops: www.energystar.gov/index.cfm?fuseaction=find_a_product.showProductGroup&pgw_code=LT.

Vendor Sustainability Index   When selecting an eco-friendly desktop/laptop vendor, reports will assist your effort. Technology Business Research announced that Dell took the number-one position in its inaugural Corporate Sustainability Index Benchmark Report for 2009, shown in Figure 2.5. The report measures the environmental initiatives of 37 companies in the computer hardware, software, professional services, and network and telecommunications sectors. Scoring 317.9 points, Dell led the second place firm (BT) by more than 52 points in the overall index ranking. The report scored more than 100 discrete sustainability factors, including emissions, energy, renewable energy, annualized emission reductions, water use, recycling rates, public environmental commitments, and more.[6]

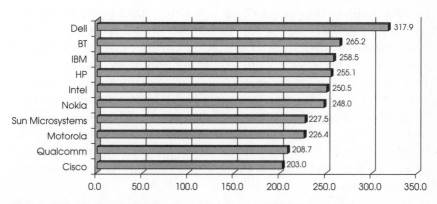

Figure 2.5   Technology Business Research 2009 Corporate Sustainability Index Scores

Source: TBR, © 2009

EPP   Environmentally Preferable Purchasing (EPP) helps the U.S. federal government "buy green," and in doing so, uses the federal government's enormous buying power to stimulate market demand for green products and services. Geared first to help federal purchasers, this site can help green vendors, businesses large and small, and consumers. Use the easy index to:

- Find and evaluate information about green products and services
- Identify federal green buying requirements
- Calculate the costs and benefits of purchasing choices
- Manage green purchasing processes

Environmentally Preferable

Products or services that have a lesser or reduced effect on human health and the environment when compared with competing products or services that serve the same purpose. This comparison applies to raw materials, manufacturing, packaging, distribution, use, reuse, operation, maintenance, and disposal.

Source: U.S. Government – Instructions for Implementing Executive Order 13423

Part of the EPP, the EPEAT (Electronic Products Environmental Assessment Tool) system can aid in the selection of eco-friendly desktop/laptop vendors. EPEAT is a system that helps purchasers evaluate, compare, and select electronic products based on their environmental attributes. It currently covers desktop and laptop computers, thin clients, and computer monitors. Desktops, laptops, and monitors that meet 23 required environmental performance criteria may be registered in EPEAT by their manufacturers. Registered products are rated Gold, Silver, or Bronze, depending on the percentage of 28 optional criteria they meet above the baseline criteria. EPEAT operates an ongoing verification program to ensure the credibility of the registry.[7] Further information is at www.epeat.net/

Server Virtualization   Server virtualization has become a mainstream offering and a necessity in many organizations that require a reduction in the number of physical servers in data centers, with the goal of reducing data center resource requirements, especially power consumption and cooling. Server virtualization offers flexibility in server deployment and in the deployment and life cycle of applications. IT professionals deploy and use virtualization to consolidate workloads and reduce server sprawl. Additionally, they use virtualization with clustering technologies to provide a robust IT infrastructure with high availability and quick disaster recovery. IT professionals increasingly look to live migration to create a dynamic and flexible IT environment that responds to emerging business needs.

Each traditional physical server in an organization's infrastructure creates a guaranteed minimum power usage overhead, dictated by the power supply, physical devices (e.g., hard disks) connected to the server, cooling requirements, and other factors. This minimum can account for 60% or more of the server's maximum power draw, even when the server is idle. However, servers typically run at far below their capacity and on average utilize only 5% to 15% of the actual capabilities of the central processing unit (CPU). This low asset utilization is a problem created by a number of factors, such as lack of flexibility in utilizing computing resources and the difficulty in estimating how much capacity will be needed. Traditionally, most organizations allocate processing power, storage, and memory resources in order to handle anticipated peak loads and unanticipated usage spikes, rather than for normal operating requirements. The result is an excess of capacity during periods of normal operation. In addition, when buying servers, a company may buy more processing power than needed because its choices are limited; for example, less powerful processors may no longer be available, or local policy dictates minimum requirements for the organization. The result is an excess of capacity that is effectively wasted during periods of normal operation.

An example of a server virtualization product is the Microsoft Windows 2008 R2 Hyper-V offering. Hyper-V provides a dynamic, reliable, and scalable virtualization platform combined with a single set of integrated management tools to manage both physical and virtual resources, enabling you to create an agile and dynamic data center. Hyper-V offers these eco-friendly features:

- **Server consolidation**. Businesses are under pressure to ease management and reduce costs while retaining and enhancing competitive advantages, such as flexibility, reliability, scalability, and security. The fundamental use of virtualization to help consolidate many servers on a single system while maintaining isolation helps address these demands. One of the main benefits of server consolidation is a lower total cost of ownership, not just from lowering hardware requirements but also from lower power, cooling, and management costs. Businesses also benefit from server virtualization through infrastructure optimization, from an asset utilization standpoint and from the ability to balance workloads across different resources. Improved flexibility of the overall environment and the ability to freely integrate 32-bit and 64-bit workloads in the same environment is another benefit.

- **Testing and development**. Testing and development frequently are the first business functions to take advantage of virtualization technology. Using virtual machines, development staffs can create and test a wide variety of scenarios in a safe, self-contained environment that accurately approximates the operation of physical servers and clients, thus reducing physical server deployments. Hyper-V maximizes utilization of test hardware, which can help reduce costs, improve life cycle management, and improve test coverage. With extensive guest operating system support and checkpoint features, Hyper-V provides a great platform for test and development environments.

- **Cost reductions**. Data centers with multiple Hyper-V physical hosts can service those systems in a controlled fashion, scheduling maintenance during regular business hours. Live migration makes it possible to keep virtual machines (VMs) online, even during maintenance, increasing productivity for users and server administrators. Data centers can now also reduce power consumption by dynamically increasing consolidation ratios and powering off unused physical hosts during lower demand times.

- **Power consumption reductions**. Hyper-V in Windows Server 2008 R2 adds enhancements that reduce virtual machine power consumption. Hyper-V now supports Second Level Address Translation, which uses new features on today's CPUs to improve VM performance while reducing processing load on the Windows Hypervisor. New Hyper-V VMs also consume less power by virtue of the new Core Parking feature implemented in Windows Server 2008 R2.

Storage Virtualization   Storage virtualization makes it possible for systems to access a shared storage subsystem that is somewhere out on the net. By tightly integrating server and storage virtualization, you can support hundreds of virtual machines while allocating storage and provisioning servers in just minutes, in addition to scaling as needed.

Files that used to be stored on every computer's disks can now be stored once in the shared storage subsystem. Storage virtualization can reduce the number of storage devices needed, the amount of power required, the heat produced and, as a wonderful side effect, would reduce the operational and administrative costs of back up, archival storage and the like. Storage virtualization can help organizations reduce hardware, maintenance and administrative costs.[8]

Cloud Computing   Cloud computing is taking hold as a service offering that will offer a computing model to assist with the explosive growth of IT resources that are Internet connected. Information technology is changing rapidly and now forms an invisible layer that increasingly touches every aspect of our lives. Power grids, traffic control, healthcare, water supplies, food and energy, and most of the world's financial transactions—all now depend on IT.

Cloud Computing

According to the Gartner Group, cloud computing is "a style of computing where massively scalable IT-related capabilities are provided 'as a service' to multiple external customers using Internet technologies."
Source: www.gartner.com/it/page.jsp?id=707508

Cloud computing concepts include:

- Virtualization and automation
- Interchangeable (fungible) resources such as servers, storage, and network
- Management of these resources as a single fabric
- Elastic capacity (scale up or down) to respond to business demands

- Applications (and the tools to develop them) that can truly scale out
- Focus on the service delivered to the business
- Reduction of physical servers

Cloud services operating systems, such as Microsoft Windows Azure, serve as a development, service hosting, and service management environment that provides developers with on-demand computing and storage to host, scale, and manage Web applications on the Internet.

Reducing the number of hardware components and replacing them with cloud computing systems reduces energy costs for running hardware and cooling, as well as reducing carbon dioxide emissions and conserving energy. These reductions can also work in combination with government tax incentives, thus offering encouragement to organizations to go and stay Green.

An example of a Green-related application running in a cloud is the Microsoft Hohm application, which is built on the Windows Azure cloud operating system and leverages Bing search as well as the Microsoft Advertising platform, and is accessible from any computer using a modern browser. Microsoft Hohm is a new online application that enables consumers to better understand their energy usage, get recommendations, and start saving money. Microsoft Hohm, name was chosen because it is a play on the words "home" and "ohm" which is a measurement unit in the energy field uses advanced analytics licensed from the Lawrence Berkeley National Laboratory and the U.S. Department of Energy to provide consumers with personalized energy-saving recommendations. Microsoft Hohm is an easy-to-use tool that helps consumers lower their energy bills and reduce their impact on the environment. The beta application is available at no cost to anyone in the United States with an Internet connection and can be accessed directly by visiting www.microsoft-hohm.com.

Wireless Networks and Mobile Devices   The proliferation of mobile devices is causing networks and data centers to grow to accommodate wireless networking, adding to overall power consumption. Laptops and the mobile phones/PDAs are wireless and mobile devices that organizations need to address in their Green initiatives. These devices create e-waste; thus there arises the Green-related concern of recycling mobile devices and batteries.

Some Greening tips for mobile devices and networks that can assist an organization in their Green initiatives are listed next.

- Improve wireless network efficiency.
- Choose a vendor with lowest power and smallest footprint per unit.
- Increase average replacement cycle to between 12 and 18 months, with special attention to the Greening efforts of mobile device manufacturers.
- Stay aware of governmental regulations and initiatives (i.e., battery directives, International Organization for Standardization [ISO] standards).
- Implement an assessment and procurement process that encourages solar handsets, handset recycling, awareness for Green handsets, take-back and recycling, and so on.

IT Offerings

Beyond the human resources and technology of an IT department are what is considered its offerings: skill sets, capabilities, and functionality that the department offers the organization to assist with business challenges and needs. IT offerings work with strategic information systems that are aligned to assist with the organization's strategic objectives. It is not that strategic information systems are essentially different applications; their impact on the business due to the changes they enable or cause is different.[9] It is this impact that is of value to organizational Green initiatives.

These offerings are defined in a way that the business can relate to and map to its needs, thus removing much of techie terms and IT jargon. Some examples of offerings that can be mapped to Green initiatives include:

- Green IT assessment, procurement, and advising
- Asset management
- Application portfolio management
- Application development
- IT-business application architecture and planning
- IT systems and data center architecture and management
- Enterprise data management/master data management
- Tactical, operational, and strategic reporting

- Business intelligence analytics and predictive analysis
- Knowledge management
- Collaboration and content management
- Business performance management
- Auditing and regulatory compliance
- Video-conferencing and communication
- Project management

The IT department strives to look for ways to reduce operational costs, one of which is energy costs for IT equipment, data centers, cooling, and more. Thus, many IT departments have years of experience assessing and procuring energy-efficient equipment and in designing and building of data centers. An organization can benefit from this experience in Green initiatives that utilize the same principles but with other types of equipment.

Additionally, the selection of Green IT vendors is of considerable importance in the procurement process, as is IT department assessments of Green IT technologies offered now and five years, ten years, and farther into the future. These IT assessment practices can be a model for the rest of the organization. The IT department typically works with Green associations in conferences, seminars, using training material and communicating with others in the IT community.

The IT department can be a very productive advisor to the rest of the organization with respect to Green technology assessment and procurement. Utilize this department from the very beginning of your Green initiative efforts.

Systems and Data Center Design and Management

New data center projects are taking a closer look at renewable energy sources, including solar and wind, as a way to improve corporate sustainability and cut energy use. Solar panels can be installed on the roofs of data centers, organizations can work with local power companies in the creation and use of renewable energy sources, and firms can purchase only renewable energy power for the data center.

IT departments can offer system management and architecture assistance. This is where the design of IT and computer systems are reviewed from top to bottom to determine options, abilities, and

Data Center Design and Management: Green Example

Microsoft's Global Foundation Services'(GFS) team is taking these significant steps to environmental sustainability:

- **Using recycled resources whenever practical.** The Microsoft data center in San Antonio, Texas, for example, uses approximately 8 million gallons of recycled water a month from the city's wastewater system during peak cooling months.
- **Using renewable resources whenever available.** The Microsoft data center in Quincy, Washington, uses 100% renewable hydropower from the Columbia Basin River. The San Antonio facility obtains its electricity from a utility that derives more than 10% of its peak capacity from renewable energy, including wind, solar, and landfill gas. And the Dublin, Ireland, data center will use outside air for cooling, thereby reducing the need for energy-intensive coolers.
- Microsoft has also implemented a number of best practices and policy guidelines that drive its construction and facility operations worldwide. Examples include benchmarks for the design, construction, and operation of high performance green buildings, high efficiency electric motors for pumps and fans, electronic variable speed drives, electronic ballasts for fluorescent lamps, and occupancy dimmers. In short, GFS leaves no stone unturned in optimizing its use of power and natural resources.

Source: www.microsoft.com/environment/our_commitment/articles/datacenter_bp.aspx

modifications that could be implemented to assist with Green initiatives. Such systems include enterprise resource planning (ERP), supply chain, manufacturing, logistics, and more. These systems could be localized and/or implemented globally across many different business areas, utilizing vast amounts of human, technical, and natural resources. Thus, reviewing these systems to make them more energy efficient and in line with Green initiatives is crucial. Furthermore, these systems can assist business functions in general in becoming Greener: Streamlining the supply chain processes and systems required to perform them could reduce resource needs that in effect reduce energy consumption (i.e., improving shipping and transport of goods and products that reduces fossil fuel consumption).

Performance Dashboards and Scorecards

The tracking and reporting of Green initiatives can be done through the application development IT offering of tactical, operational, and strategic reporting and/or business intelligence analytics and predictive analysis. One such example is the implementation of a dashboard with a scorecard and associated reports, offered by Microsoft with the Environmental Sustainability Dashboard (shown in Figure 2.6) for Microsoft Dynamics AX. It helps businesses automatically collect the data they need so they can understand their environmental impact. To facilitate environmental awareness, business processes, such as accounts payable, inventory management, and expense management, have been extended to include

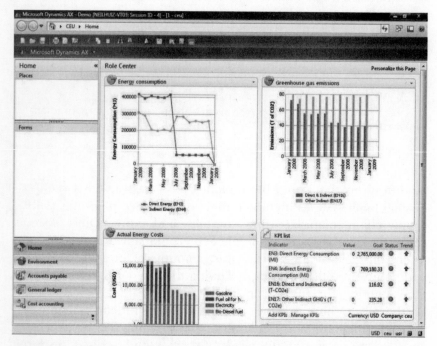

Figure 2.6   Microsoft Dynamics AX Dashboard

the automatic collection of relevant environmental data. These data are used to monitor energy consumption and greenhouse gas emissions.

The data from the dashboard can help businesses become aware—often for the first time—of their environmental impact. With this knowledge, they can choose to implement environmentally sustainable business policies and practices. After these policies and practices are in place, businesses can use the Environmental Sustainability Dashboard to track and display their effects.

Because the data are gathered and stored in the Microsoft Dynamics AX database, the information can be shared throughout an organization. The dashboard components are Microsoft SharePoint Web parts that can be propagated in Microsoft Dynamics AX Role Centers and on any enterprise portal site. This capability provides companies with a great deal of flexibility regarding who views environmental information.[10]

Videoconferencing

Videoconferencing technology gives moderators the ability to control attendance, time, content, and frequency of meetings. This communication tool allows moderators the freedom to invite participants of their choice and to deny access to others. In addition, moderators are able effectively to shadow and monitor conversations between other participants in the meetings. Depending on the software utilized, videoconferencing technology gives moderators the unique ability to integrate scheduling requirements with automated email functions. Moderators can organize unlimited future teleconferencing virtual board meetings prior to the actual dates of the conference.

Recent important technological improvements in videoconferencing include:

- Broader connection
- Increased quality of flat screens and cameras
- Multisite collaborating in meetings
- Dynamic placement of camera on the person talking during a videoconference in the conference room

Consultation advisory emails are followed up by automated responses from intended participants well in advance of planned meetings so there is never any guessing as to who will attend and how long they will participate at any given time.

Enhanced videoconference service is an easily managed module. It enables moderators to achieve their business goals via the well-oiled machinery of enhanced communication, which ultimately offers them the opportunity to dedicate their expertise to the business's other most valuable commodity: time.

In addition to increasing productivity and communications within the company, videoconferencing provides tangible savings in time that previously would be spent in airports and hotels, not to mention the costs of airline tickets and room accommodations. With today's unpredictable airline security issues, videoconferencing enables participants to avoid many problems.

With less travel, more opportunity to share and coordinate information globally, and the ability to monitor and control various aspects of a far-reaching field of command, an effective manager will soon see the benefits of video teleconferencing.

Another major advantage of a videoconference is the ease with which people outside of an organization can join in. Say, for example, you are involved in building projects. Chances are that a different architect is used for each project. If your meeting requires the presence of a nonemployed expert, it is far easier to organize if you are running a videoconference rather than a meeting in the flesh.

Videoconferencing: Green Example

TNT is a worldwide operating company with an active global network. Across the world, around the clock, TNT delivers millions of parcels, documents, and freight shipments to customers in more than 200 countries. The base of its success and leadership position in the industry depends largely on the engagement of TNT's 161,000 employees. TNT has set up videoconferencing systems around the world with the expectation of reducing its business travel by 20% and saving €3.2 million annually. On top of reducing travel costs and carbon dioxide emissions, videoconferencing should also increase productivity, reduce travel time, allow a better work-life balance, and improve motivation (more people able to participate in meetings).

Source: http://group.tnt.com/career/workingattnt/index.aspx

Custom Application Development

Custom application development offerings can allow an organization to measure, track, and report the objectives, goals, status, costs, and other environmental and economic KPIs that will assist Green initiative efforts. It is here that IT department application developers can create custom tools for the organization specific to Green initiatives. This can be done via a custom Balanced Scorecard application, custom report development, creation of custom add-ins and enhancements to off-the-shelf products, and much more.

The Clinton Foundation and Microsoft will be assisted in developing new measurement tools by ICLEI-Local Governments for Sustainability and the Center for Neighborhood Technology. Microsoft will build the new software tools using the knowledge base that ICLEI has acquired in developing its Harmonized Emissions Analysis Tool. The role of communities in tackling carbon emissions is vital. The Clinton Foundation and Microsoft believe technology can play a unique role in bringing people together to tackle the global environmental challenges that the world faces today. The partnership aims to empower cities with relevant technology to address shared global environmental issues. Microsoft, together with a consortium of partners, will develop a single Web solution, shown in Figure 2.7, named Project 2°, that will allow cities to clearly understand their environmental footprint. With this information, cities can make better choices as they aim to improve their energy efficiency and reduce carbon emissions.

As part of their partnership combining cutting-edge technology and environmental data, Microsoft and the European Environment Agency (EEA) have recently expanded the Eye On Earth portal. A new application, AirWatch, provides information on air quality to more than 500 million people in 32 countries across Europe. For the first time, EEA brings together both measured and modeled data alongside citizens' observations on air quality.

Eye On Earth was first launched in May 2008 with WaterWatch, an application presenting water-quality data on an interactive site powered by Bing Maps. With this new update, Eye On Earth gets not just a fresh look and feel for both air and bathing water information; it also becomes one of the newest applications built on Windows Azure and SQL Azure hosting the Geo Observatory Data Store. The site's user interface provides interactive information from Europe-wide to street level, based on data from water- and

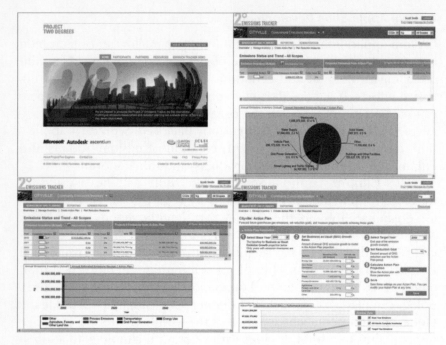

Figure 2.7   Custom Application: Project 2°

air-quality measurement stations and citizens' input. It translates scientific data into easily understandable terms and makes it available in 24 languages.

In addition to near-real-time data on specific air pollutants available from air-quality measurement stations, AirWatch presents air-quality information based on Europe-wide modeling covering larger areas. This allows users to get an indication of the air quality anywhere in Europe, not only near measurement stations. Users will also see how other viewers describe the air in a particular area.[11]

Tactical, Operational, and Strategic Reporting

There exists a need for many Green initiatives to report their efforts, progress, and results to corporate leaders, management, customers, investors, and regulators. Typically IT has deployed enterprise reporting systems that can fulfill the reporting needs of environmental sustainability requirements and Green initiative efforts.

Not only do organizations have to report on Green initiative efforts internally to manage the progress; they also must supply data to government regulators to ensure compliance with laws. Thus firms have an even stronger need for an effective enterprise reporting system.

An enterprise reporting system should be easy to deploy and use in order to benefit the organization quickly and effectively. Some characteristics of an enterprise reporting system that can help with environmentally sustainability compliance and Green initiative efforts are listed next.

- Internet, extranet, and intranet reporting abilities
- Operational and production reporting
- Analytic and strategic reporting
- Business reporting
- Central reporting repositories to create one final version of reports
- Multilingual support
- Ad hoc reporting capabilities
- Exporting of report content
- Secured reporting abilities
- Heterogeneous report data source selection
- Environmental sustainability compliance report templates and adherence to reporting standards and requirements

Data Mining, Predictive Analysis, and Forecasting

A result of implementing information systems such as regulatory compliance systems, environmental management systems, and enterprise resource planning or customer relationship management applications to automate business processes is the accumulation of vast amounts of data. Implementation reporting environments go beyond traditional transactional reporting and use of the data; they include operational data stores, data warehouses, and data marts to assimilate data from disparate operating systems and applications. These reporting environments are extremely beneficial to individuals who need to obtain timely and accurate information for decision-making purposes. Methods of accessing information from these reporting environments range from ad hoc queries to multidimensional analysis. While these forms of data analysis are excellent at answering questions posed by information consumers, they do not provide any other insight.

Individuals and organizations are recognizing that additional value may lie within the vast amounts of data that they are storing. By applying data mining techniques, which combine elements of statistics, artificial intelligence, and machine learning, they are able to identify trends within the data that they did not know existed. Data mining can best be described as a business intelligence (BI) technology that uses various techniques to extract comprehensible, hidden, and useful information from a population of data. This BI technology makes it possible to discover hidden trends and patterns in large amounts of data. The output of a data mining exercise can take the form of patterns, trends, or rules that are implicit in the data. Through data mining and the new knowledge it provides, individuals are able to create new opportunities or value for their organizations.

SAS Institute Inc. offers a product titled SAS for Sustainability Management that will assist organizations in predicting and responding to environmental, social, and economic risks and opportunities.[12] Organizational performance now requires sustainability measures across social, environmental, and economic factors, which in turn requires the vital steps of integrating and analyzing data to achieve new goals and transform internal organizational cultures. The most strategic enterprises will use data, and the intelligence gained from it, to their competitive advantage—driving increased brand value through innovation, improving internal efficiencies and accountability, and engendering loyalty of consumers, employees, and other stakeholders. SAS for Sustainability Management enables an organization to measure, manage, and report on the Triple Bottom Line—environmental, social, and economic indicators—and determine business strategies that reduce risk and increase shareholder value. With SAS, organizations can:

- **Measure key sustainability activities** using industry-accepted methodologies and protocols via data integration and analytic capabilities, which leverage existing investments in operational systems and databases.
- **Report ongoing performance** to ensure transparency with key stakeholders and compliance with regulatory agencies. By establishing an integrated, consistent source of quality information, organizations can bind initiatives to a common sustainability framework that allows alignment across all lines

of business—from the water treatment facility to the data center.

- **Improve performance** by identifying the metrics that have the greatest impact on goal attainment so organizations can make the most informed strategic decisions. Apply SAS optimization, forecasting, and data mining capabilities to analyze scenarios and run simulations to improve response and successful strategy execution.
- **Manage and forecast** the finances and resources needed to achieve the desired outcomes across the enterprise and within each department. Prioritize organizational strategies and align investments in new product innovation, program development, and talent accordingly. Establish scorecards and strategy maps driven by the sustainability goals of the organization.

Summary

This chapter offers insights into the value and benefits of integrating the IT department's resources and offerings into the organization's Green initiatives. It is crucial for an organization to maximize IT department human and technical resources to provide the maximum benefit to its Green initiatives. The IT department can offer Green advising due to experiences in Greening IT. IT departments have many Green-related technologies and processes to make then eco-friendly and to assist the organization in its overall environmental sustainability goals. Thus, it is not difficult to see that the IT department and environmental sustainability go hand and hand within an organization. Additionally, the need to integrate the IT department into an organization's Green initiatives may be due to external forces (i.e., government regulations, Green consumer demands, etc.). IT department offerings can assist here with external environmental sustainability compliance reporting to government agencies and Green consumer portals, providing information on the organization's environmentally sustainable efforts, performance metrics, compliance, and more.

Furthermore, organizations should strive to find ways to improve and enhance this IT-business alignment and integration in its Green initiatives to assist with many other organizational strategic goals: increasing competitiveness, social responsibility, and customer satisfaction.

Notes

1. C. Hill, *Global Business Today* (New York: McGraw-Hill Irwin, 2008).
2. S. P. Robbins, *Essentials of Organization Behavior* (8th ed.) (Upper Saddle River, NJ: Prentice Hall, 2005).
3. http://greeninc.blogs.nytimes.com/2009/03/02/companies-add-chief-sustainability-officers/
4. www.longbeach.gov/civica/filebank/blobdload.asp?BlobID=23282
5. Environmental Protection Agency, EPA Report to Congress on Server and Data Center Energy Efficiency, 2007; www.energystar.gov/ia/partners/prod_development/downloads/EPA_Report_Exec_Summary_Final.pdf
6. www.tbri.com/news/pressreleases.cfm
7. www.epeat.net/default.aspx
8. Kusnetzky, D. (May 2007). Storage virtualization and green computing. www.zdnet.com/blog/virtualization/storage-virtualization-and-green-computing/142
9. J. Ward and J. Peppard, *Strategic Planning for Information Systems* (Hoboken: NJ: John Wiley & Sons, 2002).
10. Additional information can be found at these Web sites: www.microsoft.com/environment/business_solutions/articles/dynamics_ax.aspx; www.microsoft.com/dynamics/en/us/environment.aspx
11. http://eyeonearth.cloudapp.net/
12. www.sas.com/solutions/sustainability

CHAPTER 3

Green Initiative Strategy with IT

This chapter offers strategy concepts, tools, and a framework that can be implemented by organizations beginning or modifying their Green initiative efforts. As information technology (IT) department resources are of great value to many organizational Green initiative efforts, it is appropriate to have the organization's Green initiative strategy integrate IT department resources and offerings in a cohesive and integrated manner. This forms IT-enabled business programs, which can benefit from the strategic IT-business relationship, IT cross-functional business operations, and IT offerings integrated into key strategic projects, products, and services that are to be impacted by the Green initiative efforts.

Furthermore, the Green initiatives are not designed and formulated at a department or project level but must fit within the strategic vision and goals of an organization. Thus, organization-wide implementation is required to align the Green initiative strategy with overall organizational strategic goals.

Strategy maps are used to help visualize the organization's Green initiative strategy with respect to objectives, dependencies, interrelationships, and more. Ensure your strategy is sound, decisive, actionable, and achievable. The value of strategy maps is enhanced with a defined and well-thought-out organizational plan to achieve its mission. Additionally, strategy mapping can assist with communication and execution of the chosen plan.

Figure 3.1 offers insight into a formula that helps show how strategy mapping and IT department integration combined with

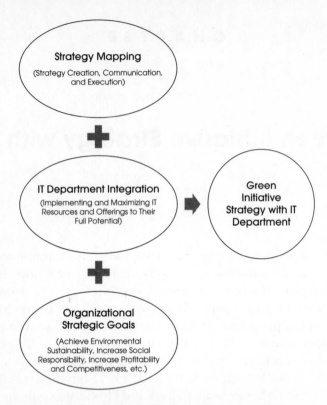

Figure 3.1   Formula for Green Initiative Strategy with IT

organizational strategic goals can lead to a Green initiative strategy with the IT department.

Strategy Mapping + IT Department Integration + Organizational Strategic Goals = Green Initiative Strategy with IT Department

Strategy Mapping

Strategy mapping is a technique of providing a visual representation of the links among the different components of an organization's strategy. Strategy mapping can assist any size organization, from a Fortune 1 global organization to small, local organizations. No matter what the organization's size, the aim is to define strategy elements and align them to the organization's core strategic goals. Emphasis is placed on communicating the strategy to others and tracking strategy execution using a business scorecard.

Before creating a strategy map, ensure you have a well-defined, focused, and complete strategy that has been reviewed by organizational leaders. Be sure they have clarified and agreed on one interpretation of the strategy. Once you have some universal consensus, start by building a prototype strategy map that can be circulated among the organizational leaders for review, edits, comments, and finally approval. The strategy map needs to be more than a visual depiction of the strategy; it should have the ability to accelerate its execution.

The next list explains the structure of a strategy map and its constituents.

- Depiction of a table or grid, with a defined row structure.
- Each layer or row is called a perspective, which has medium-term goals, commonly called strategic objectives.
- Upward-pointing arrows are drawn between the objectives to indicate either cause and effect or strategic support. (This replaces earlier value chains, which indicated cause and effect or process flow. Many people consider the strategy map to be a group of linked or companion value chains.)
- Four common perspectives are used: Finance, Customer, Internal Business Process, and Learning and Growth.
- The top layer is often considered to be the organization's public interface. Objectives in this row should show support for the visionary goals relating to vision, mission, market, and slogan.
- Inside the map, each row is supported by the layer or row below, as indicated by the arrows.
- Strategy maps often illustrate a primary critical success factor (CSF) objective, such as a funding goal or an overall product quality issue. In this case, you would expect to see a number of arrows pointing both toward and away from any CSF objective.

PerformancePoint Services in Microsoft SharePoint Server 2010 is a tool that can be used with strategy maps and scorecards. PerformancePoint dashboards provide a report view for creating cause-and-effect diagrams using Microsoft Office Visio 2007/2010 templates and data-driven shapes linked directly to PerformancePoint KPI values and targets. Figure 3.2 shows an example of a strategy map and its associated scorecard. They identify leading indicators of strategic success and can track and score a structured set of strategic performance metrics, visible in the scorecard. The goal is

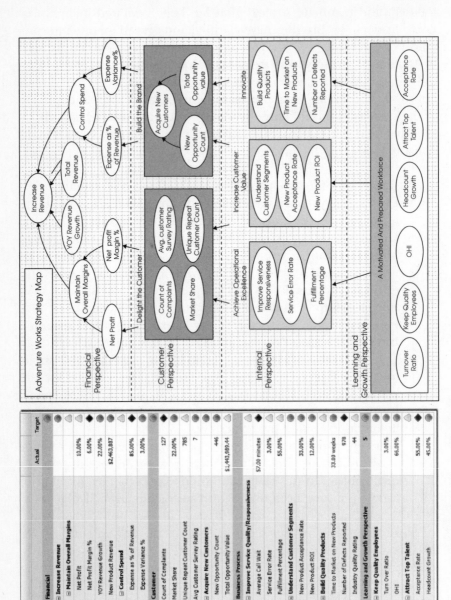

Figure 3.2 Strategy Map and Scorecard

to accelerate strategy execution by aligning organizational leaders around this visualization of the strategy and to communicate it to employees. Assistance in creating strategy maps and scorecards with Microsoft PerformancePoint Server 2007 can be found at: http://blogs.msdn.com/performancepoint/archive/2007/07/20/strategy-maps-in-performancepoint-server.aspx

Strategy Framework Components

A Green initiative strategy will require participation, collaboration, and cohesiveness of many resources to achieve maximum benefits to the organization, Green consumers, and the environment. One such necessary component is the IT department.

The strategy framework in Figure 3.3 lists key functions, subject areas, and efforts that are to be included in the strategy's mission and description. This framework shows that many key business

Figure 3.3   Green Initiative Strategy Framework that Integrates IT

operational areas are influenced and critical to the success of the strategy's effectiveness, gains, and achievements.

Executive Leadership

Green programs fail due to lack of executive buy-in, lack of accountability, and lack of measurable results. In contrast, programs with executive sponsorship are more likely to garner necessary financial and personnel resources.[1] With the success of Green initiatives hinging on having organizational strategic implementation, funding, and performance gains, executive sponsorship is not just beneficial but crucial and a necessity.

Without executive-level sponsorship, Green initiatives sink to a lower level of precedence, funding, and effectiveness for the organization as a whole. Figure 3.4 depicts the importance of executive-level participation and sponsorship of Green initiatives. In some cases, Green initiatives become department-level efforts, such as a

SAVE THE PLANET

IN YOUR BOARDROOM

Figure 3.4   Executive Sponsorship and Environmental Sustainability Integration

department recycling program. Some departments reject Green initiatives entirely and others may offer minimal effort; thus, there would be little at the organizational level to show customers, regulators, competition, and investors that the firm is a serious contributor to environmental sustainability and is acting socially responsibly.

When a Green initiative strategy has IT integration, executive sponsorship may mean that both the chief executive officer (CEO) and chief information officer (CIO) are involved, as well as assigned representatives who are involved on their behalf. These delegated representatives should have executive authority and could be in a position referred to as a chief environmental sustainability officer, vice president of IT, or something similar. This does not mean that the CEO and CIO never interact or participate in key Green initiative discussions; it means that a second in command is available to ensure that no time or momentum is lost on Green initiative efforts when the CEO or CIO is not available.

Some requirements and characteristics of a sponsor for Green initiatives are listed next.

- **Leadership**. Provides leadership, especially direction, protection, and problem-resolution skills. Sets the organization's vision and strategy for sustainability in alignment with business strategy and goals.
- **Influential**. Has influential power and can impact the success of the Green initiatives. Shapes decision making at all levels, can influence other executives and the board of directors. (Beware of sponsor with a hidden agenda to torpedo the Green initiatives; be ready to deal with negative influences as well with positive influences.) Mobilizes and aligns other key business leaders and stakeholders, so they can propagate sustainability initiatives through the organization.
- **Advocate and cheerleader**. Is the primary advocate of the Green initiatives by presenting, justifying, and showing strong support for a business case to organization executives that will secure funding and executive-level support. The advocacy efforts need to be visible to the participants in the Green initiative projects as well as to executive management. The executive sponsor has to motivate team members and make sure they know that their efforts are valued by upper management. In addition, the executive sponsor needs to

promote the program's progress and reaffirm its importance to any critics. This is particularly important when problems arise and additional funds are needed, which is inevitable in large efforts.

- **Be respected and valued within the organization**. Must be a respected and valued executive, not a lame duck, not retired on active duty and waiting for retirement to come, or on the chop block for dismissal. Any of those positions would weaken the executive's ability to perform.

- **Be a personal example of Green initiatives**. Must be personally eco-conscious and responsible. To be environmentally concerned only when at work will show and will negatively impact the Green initiatives within the organization. Review what the executive sponsors drive to work, what environmental actions they partake in, whether they use power-saving options on office desktop/laptop, and so on.

- **Active participation**. Is more than a casual observer. The sponsor must be an active participant who can assist in successful completion of the Green initiatives. This will not require day-to-day oversight or micromanagement, but it will be more than attending the kick-off meeting for Green initiatives and then coming back at the very end when they are finished. Sponsors must understand and commit to the responsibility of keeping the Green initiatives on schedule, on budget, and achieving their planned benefits for the organization.

- **Chair the Green initiative steering committee**. This level of participation will be extremely valuable in ensuring progress, making concessions and trade-offs, removing roadblocks, and motivating the teams. Chairing this committee will ensure that the executive sponsor is close enough to the issues to help the other executives make effective decisions.

- **Encourage risk assessment**. In major business programs, the executive sponsor may commission a project risk assessment. Although the program team frequently views risk assessments as a threat, the real goal should be risk mitigation. The point is not to cancel the project but to protect it. A risk assessment performed by an outside firm can provide an independent perspective and valuable objectivity to help prevent disasters down the road.

- **Assess and approve Green initiative deliverables**. As deliverables occur during the implementation stage of Green initiative projects, the executive sponsor will decide whether the predefined acceptance criteria have been met for each one.
- **Allocates resources**. Able to work effectively with departments within the organization to acquire members for Green initiatives project teams. This takes strong influence, justification, prioritization, time, money, and patience. Staffing of Green initiatives projects is just as important and critical as the funding of these efforts.
- **Effective communication skills**. Able to communicate effectively sincerely, both verbally and written, to other executives, employees, and board of directors on the importance of Green initiatives and the overall importance of achieving the organization's environmental sustainability goal. This communication may also reach beyond the organization to partnerships, regulators, vendors, and customers.
- **Demonstrates commitment**. Through active participation, leadership, being a personal example, and much more, the sponsor will need to demonstrate sincere and unwavering commitment to Green initiatives. The sponsor must ensure that Green initiatives remain a priority.

Practices, Policies, and Principles

Promoting sustainable business policies is part of the strategy framework that establishes an organization's commitment to a goal of sustainability. Protecting the environment makes good business sense.
    Additional concepts of these policies are listed next.

- Supply chain and manufacturing will implement programs from the Environmental Protection Agency (EPA), such as Clean Processing, Design for the Environment, and Green Suppliers Network.
- Equipment, especially IT related, will be procured that is in alignment with EPA programs such as ENERGY STAR and WaterSense.
- Office space will be leased in accordance with Green leasing guidelines, (i.e., high ENERGY STAR ratings and high level of energy efficiency).

- Organization will promote recycling and electronic waste (e-waste, e-scrap, etc.) disposal practices to the maximum extent possible.
- Green initiative efforts will emphasize social responsibility and environmental sustainability.
- Establish practices that meet or exceed relevant environmental legislation. Adhere to agreements and standards at local, national, and international levels and review voluntary agreements.
- Establish and maintain an environmental management system and audit it by means of a systematic, documented verification process to ensure continuous improvement.
- Communicate its environmental policy to employees and other stakeholders, and publish its results in environmental reports.
- Educate its employees to work within its environmental policy.

To support these policies, the organization can implement these practices:

- Preferentially select a network of vendors that have expertise in sustainable practices.
- Continually improve and upgrade water efficiency, energy utilization, and waste management within facilities.
- Maintain a high level of internal expertise regarding sustainability.
- Conduct regular financial analysis to assess the potential benefits of using or implementing more efficient equipment and practices in facilities.
- Select office and manufacturing sites that favor alternative means of transportation or shorter commuting distances for employees.
- During the site selection process, measure and evaluate a site's overall sustainability performance.
- Preferentially select buildings with high ENERGY STAR ratings.
- Promote energy efficiency.
- Use ENERGY STAR and Watersense products and equipment.
- Take advantage of the utility company's audit and incentive programs to implement cost-effective measures.
- Utilize occupancy-based lighting control systems with appropriate zoning and daylight linking.

Principles: Green Example

In 2008, 3M launched a company-wide project to develop three strategic principles around sustainability. 3M's strategies for sustainability encompass the pursuit of customer satisfaction and commercial success within a framework of environmental, social, and economic values. These principles, developed collaboratively across businesses and geographies, provide 3M businesses and corporate staff groups with a flexible framework to engage our customers and key stakeholders around sustainability. They reflect 3M's commitment to reducing its environmental footprint, operating in a socially responsible manner, and helping 3M customers address their environmental challenges via 3M's innovative products and technologies. The principles were adopted by the Corporate Operating Committee and serve as a center point of 3M's sustainability efforts going forward. 3M Sustainability Principles are:

- **Economic Success**. Build lasting customer relationships by developing differentiated, practical, and ingenious solutions to their sustainability challenges.
- **Environmental Protection**. Provide practical and effective solutions and products to address environmental challenges for ourselves and our customers.
- **Social Responsibility**. Engage key stakeholders in dialogue and take action to improve 3M's sustainability performance.

Source: http://solutions.3m.com/3MContentRetrievalAPI/BlobServlet?locale= en_US&lmd=1241194279000&assetId=1180599175067&assetType=MMM_ Image&blobAttribute=ImageFile

Business Culture Adjustment

Business cultures that have been defined and executed that do not contain environmental sustainable practices and concepts, will need to be adjusted, redefined, and in some case rebuilt from scratch. Organizations such as The Conservation Corps of Newfoundland and Labrador can offer insight into the concept of a Green business culture:

> Green business cultures recognize that all businesses depend on natural resources. While the overriding concern remains the economic viability of the enterprise, these business owners

understand that wasting resources now will have a negative impact on the company's future viability. Planning for the future involves considering environmental stewardship, the health and safety of its workers, and efficient use of raw materials and energy. Workers are aware of the company's environmental concerns and take steps to ensure that waste is reduced to a minimum. There are constant reminders of the importance of saving energy, conserving raw materials, and reducing the amount of resources used in other aspects of the company's operations. Well-established long-term goals, teamwork, and an understanding of the resource needs of the entire scope of operations characterize the day-to-day activities of the company. Employee commitment is ensured through special benefits, bonuses, and award programs.[2]

Green Business Culture

A business environment that considers the environmental consequences of all aspects of its operations that requires the commitment of all workers and is most successful when it is a team effort.

Source: Building a Green Business Culture information sheet, www.ccnl.ca/greenerfutures/pdf/building-a-green-business-culture.pdf

Achieving environmental sustainability is one of the most important priorities in today's corporate culture due to one or more contributing and beneficial factors. Environmental responsibility affects a wide range of business decisions, including IT department hardware and software purchases, IT department data center selection and implementation, manufacturing practices, energy consumption, legislative compliance, recycling, e-waste disposal, vendor selection, and Green marketing campaigns. All of these are components that factor into how an organization will strive to define its environmental sustainability strategy and redefine its business culture.

Company culture is important because it can make or break your company. Companies with an adaptive culture that is aligned to their business goals routinely outperform their competitors.

Company cultures evolve and they change over time. As employee[s] leave the company and replacements are hired the company culture will change. If it is a strong culture, it may not change much. However, since each new employee brings their own values and practices to the group[,] the culture will change, at least a little. As the company matures from a startup to a more established company, the company culture will change. As the environment in which the company operates (the laws, regulations, business climate, etc.) changes, the company culture will also change.[3]

Organizational culture changes and change management can impact, benefit, and influence strategic goals in a positive or negative manner. With respect to environmental sustainability, the need to change may be implemented proactively or reactively. A business culture that embraces environmental sustainability as a strategic goal will experience a positive change.

Implementing a Green organizational culture, with the aid and integration of the IT department, will prove to be beneficial. The organization will think and operate within Green concepts, practices, and principles. This attitude will be projected outward to competitors, regulators, and Green consumers. Green organizational cultures are less likely to be portrayed as participating in Greenwashing tactics; thus they are seen as more sincere, actionable, and socially responsible to their employees and Green consumers.

The Green culture should not be viewed as a trend, something that will not take place, or another business concept picked up in graduate school that an organization can tinker with. Rather, it is long-term effort of becoming more effective with Green initiatives to yield even better results for the organization, employees, the environment, and the community.

Consumers and Competition

An organization's Green initiative strategy should be able to deal with competitive, market, and consumer forces that can affect its competitiveness, profitability, and image. Marketing and projecting a very sincere environmental sustainability image to Green consumers and employees can enhance an organization's image, thus possibly attracting more consumers, which in turn increases the organization's sales, profitability, and competiveness.

Actually being Green is not as easy as merely projecting an eco-friendly image to consumers. Yet these Greenwashing efforts eventually will lead to the organization being identified as a fraud. There must be long-term commitment, external eco-friendly

Business Culture: Green Examples

Interface Flooring is a world leader in the development of a Green business culture. They have proven that substantial profit increases can occur when there is a companywide, coordinated approach to Greening a business culture. Interface reduced consumption per unit produced by 70% and saved the company $3 million in energy, water, and waste disposal costs.

Another example is in Scottish Tourism case studies. Small changes around their business helped them recover money that had previously been lost as wasted materials or wasted energy. An investment of about $70 Canadian to purchase Eco-Balls instead of detergent reduced the Lochside Bed and Breakfast energy and water consumption. A small family-owned printing company, Cedar Press, made recycling a routine, and diverted nearly half their waste from the landfill. Savings totaled over $4,000 in Canadian dollars. Each of these (organizations) gain financially while at the same time reducing their impact on the environment.

Source: Building a Green Business Culture information sheet, www.ccnl.ca/greenerfutures/pdf/building-a-green-business-culture.pdf

actions, and implementation of organization-wide Green initiatives. Both employees and consumers must sense that the organization is sincere, ethical, and socially responsible in its environmentally sustainable strategy. From this comes the gains that are there for the taking. New markets, enhancing one's position in existing markets, and increasing the marketability of one's products and services are just a few potential benefits of pursuing a strategy that aligns with what consumers, government regulations, and the health of the world are all demanding.

Green consumers are well-informed consumers who are emerging as a new force in the global struggle to create an environmentally sustainable world, reports a new study by the WorldWatch Institute, a Washington, DC–based environmental and social policy research organization.[4] Green consumers are demanding from organizations:

- Larger selection of eco-friendly products and services that is as competitive in pricing, availability, usability, supportability, and reliability as products that are not eco-friendly.

- Socially responsible and ethical eco-friendly organizations pursuing environmental sustainability as a strategic goal and long-term commitment to the community, environment, and its employees.
- Pursuing compliance with environmental laws, regulations, and recommendations not only on a mandatory basis but, more important, on a voluntarily basis. Additionally, compliance is not only to meet the minimum that is required but to exceed requirements.

Additionally, there is a shift from irresponsible consumption from businesses, governments, and consumers to more environmentally sustainable economic, manufacturing, and consumer purchasing practices. If humanity is to thrive long into the future, we'll need to orient our cultures on sustainability, not consumerism.[5]

With Green consumerism on the rise, as well as marketing efforts geared specifically to the needs and purchasing power of these consumers, your organization may find that there is no better time than the present to pursue products and services that will entice Green consumers. This is very much the case with computer manufacturers that are marketing eco-friendly desktops and laptops and IT vendors that are offering software products and services to assist organizations to reach their sustainability goals while at the same time having strong and productive eco-friendly efforts within their own businesses.

Most likely, you will find that competition in your business sector may be ahead of you and has already started Green marketing campaigns and introducing products and services to Green consumers. For some organizations, knowledge that this is true may be enough to start the Green machine in motion.

Look for opportunities to be a leader. It is generally more effective to be an early adopter of a new technology or environmental practice than to be a later follower.[6] Additionally, getting ahead of your competition can be beneficial with respect to securing grants and winning competitions being held across the globe to entice citizens, organizations, and governments to present their Green ideas and projects.

One example of Green competition is in the home improvement and supplies business sector. Some companies in the space are offering eco-friendly products alongside products that are not at all environmental friendly, thus sending mixed messages to consumers.

Competition: Green Example

Green Depot's mission is to make Green building and living solutions accessible, affordable, and gratifying. Founded in November 2005, Green Depot is a leading supplier of environmentally friendly and sustainable building products, services, and solutions. Its primary goal is to facilitate Green living and building in communities. Green Depot has showrooms in Brooklyn, Newark (NJ), Philadelphia, Boston, Greenport, Chicago, Albany, and Newark (DE), a new flagship retail location in Manhattan, and 10 additional distribution centers spanning the Northeast. Each of Green Depot's products is accompanied by an icon depicting whether it is a locally produced material, made by a socially responsible company, conserves energy, or benefits air quality. This allows the shopper to make informed decisions quickly.

Source: www.greendepot.com/greendepot/

Taking this to the level where all products will be eco-friendly is a company called Green Depot.

Organizational Changes

The time has come for organizations to be reshaped, redrawn, reorganized, and redefined. This is not a new concept; throughout the twentieth century, this has occurred numerous times. One such noticeable period where IT was heavily involved was the dot.com era. This was the time when e-commerce and many other types of e-business capabilities arose, thus reshaping the business environment and organizational functionality.

For those who are prepared to act with purpose and direction in reshaping the organizational world, this is an exciting time in human history, for it is a time for the creation of innovative institutional forms to provide us all with a quality of economic, social, and cultural life that nurtures and develops our human capabilities.[7] The reshaping and redefining of an organization will include human resource management, retraining, executive rethinking, and new management styles to take an organization into the new competitive landscape that is already being defined and in many ways already being implemented. Management and those who are in leadership positions will find a new set of challenges and opportunities as the adoption, necessity, and economic benefits of environmental sustainability continue to grow. This is being seen in MBA graduate degree programs, such as the one at Cornell University Johnson School Center for Sustainable Global Enterprise, which believes the private sector "has a critical role to play in helping solve the world's most pressing environmental and social problems" by "working directly with companies around the world to identify, understand, and capitalize on these competitive opportunities."[8]

Harvard University offers the Organizational Change Management for Sustainability course, which aims to address the real-life challenges of environmental sustainability by building change agent capacities of students who operate within myriad institutional and other contexts. The course explores the wide range of institutionally related environmental impacts and roles of individuals within these settings. Additionally, Harvard offers a graduate program in Sustainability and Environmental Management at www.extension.harvard.edu/envr/.

The organizational changes should reflect a strategy that will be aligned and complement the strategic goals of the organization, adopt environmental sustainability across the entire organization, and integrate the use of the IT department as a viable and productive organizational resource in Green initiatives.

Organizational structure changes will also include the creation of environmental sustainability committees, subcommittees, virtual teams, centers of excellence, and the like. HSBC has created the Climate Change Center of Excellence, which reports jointly to the head of Global Research and the head of Group Sustainable Development, with the goal of evaluating the implications of climate change for the HSBC Group, its Global Research division, and other business units while studying the scientific, regulatory, and economic dimensions of climate change.[9]

Business Process Reengineering

Like all reengineering efforts, Green reengineering initiatives challenge the underlying organizational values and culture by changing them in the process. Green reengineering will radically change core and supporting business processes to achieve dramatic improvements in an organization's environmental sustainability goals. Green reengineering fundamentally shifts corporate valuation of its outputs to customers and to the environment. The community and the natural environment surrounding the corporation become highly prized constituencies.[10]

Green Reengineering

The application of business process reengineering concepts that consider environmental impact, by, for example, proactively redesigning and radically improving manufacturing, packaging, and distribution processes to become more sensitive to the natural environment.
Source: Adapted from www.unm.edu/~rattner/picmet97.pdf

Business process reengineering (BPR) is a technique to help organizations fundamentally rethink how they do their work in order to dramatically improve customer service, cut operational costs, and become world-class competitors. Green reengineering is a type of BPR. A key stimulus for reengineering has been the continuing development and deployment of sophisticated information systems and networks. Another stimulus is the need for organizations to pursue environmentally sustainable goals. Thus, these two stimuli can be aligned and can assist each other during Green reengineering efforts.

Will your organization's Green reengineering efforts be proactive or reactive? Green reengineering can relate to the level of organizational environmental stewardship. Organizations that choose Green engineering simply to comply with governmental regulations—those whose efforts are reactive—will be seen as having minimal or no environmental stewardship. Those organizations that implement radical Green reengineering initiatives oriented toward Green consumers and the health and well-being of the environment and community before their own organizational needs are proactive.

As indicated in Figure 3.5, work processes, information needs, and technology are interdependent. When a reengineering project leads to new information requirements, it may be necessary to acquire new technology to support those requirements. It is important to bear in mind, however, that acquiring new IT does not constitute reengineering. Technology is an *enabler* of process reengineering, not a substitute for it. Acquiring technology in the belief that its mere presence will somehow lead to process innovation is a root cause of bad investments in information systems.[11]

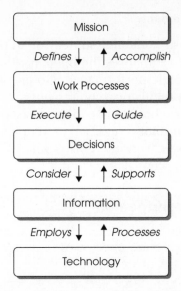

Figure 3.5   Relationship of Mission and Work Processes to Information Technology

How can IT assist in an organization's Green reengineering efforts? The IT department can contribute during the reengineering analysis and design process with graphics software and Computer-Aided Software Engineering (CASE) tools that can produce process maps; spreadsheets and costing software allow for activity-based cost analysis; databases can track customer satisfaction and complaints; "blind" e-mail bulletin boards can capture employee suggestions. In addition, e-mail and groupware can facilitate communication and coordination across geographical and organizational barriers.[12] The IT department can participate in reengineering efforts by implementing IT department–specific Green reengineering initiatives that will integrate into the organization's overall efforts and goals.

This is not to suggest that implementing IT resources, offerings, and processes is the silver bullet that will allow for new and revised business processes to achieve environmental sustainability. Rather, Green reengineering should focus on the organizational needs, business processes to create and revise, customer needs, and the strategic organizational goal requirements. From this, the IT department resources and offerings can complement, support, and enable the Green reengineering efforts with innovative, productive, and effective options.

Performance Improvements

The environmental sustainability strategy of an organization should have within its Green initiatives the mission to increase the organization's overall strategic performance. Green initiatives should do more than just satisfy regulatory requirements or some other minimal need. Green initiatives should strive to increase competiveness, profitability, social responsibility, regulatory compliance, organizational performance, and much more. This is where the value of Green initiatives has its full potential.

Performance Management

A continuous process of identifying, measuring, and developing the performance of individuals and teams and aligning performance with the strategic goals of the organizations.

Source: H. Aguinis, *Performance Management* (Upper Saddle River, NJ: Prentice Hall, 2007).

To allow for Green initiatives to be a strategic organizational benefit enabler, the organization will need to have an integrated performance management system, as shown in Figure 3.6, and practices that will invoke performance enablers and manage them with effective monitoring and scorecarding throughout the organization. The components of the integrated performance management system relate the strategic plan and the performance plan to the everyday operations plan. The guidelines and governance is via the requirements document, and the performance scorecard offers a visual representation of the progress and status of performance indicators. Admittedly, achieving a balanced, systematic, and integrated approach to organizational performance is not an easy task, yet it is absolutely vital if organizations are to navigate their way through ever-changing internal and external environmental conditions and the potential dangers that lurk within such environments.[13]

Increasing the performance of individuals and the organization as a whole is in alignment with the abilities of IT resources and offerings. In many organizations, a mandate reflects the need for IT investments to show returns on investment and to increase the performance and productivity of those utilizing the investments in daily operations and in strategic thinking and planning. Not only

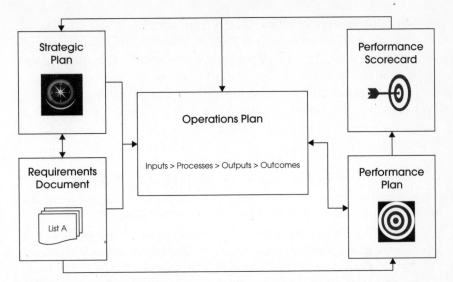

Figure 3.6   Integrated Performance Management System Conceptual Model

Source: J. Harbour, "Integrated Performance Management: A Conceptual, System-Based Model," *ISPI Journal* 48, no. 7 (August 2009): 10–14.

are IT investments internal performance enhancers, they also can enhance the performance of those external to organizations, such as partners and customers, as well. Customers have benefited from the IT investments of organizations, especially in online activities for e-commerce, online banking, and much more that allow for increases in personal and small-business productivity. Spending time driving to a bank and waiting in long lines offers little value to one's performance; the ability to log in from the convenience of one's home, business, or mobile devices to take care of banking needs with a slew of options and functionality can allow one to perform these tasks with greater efficiency, ability, and capabilities.

Now let's relate this directly to Green initiatives and the need to establish environmental sustainability via a Green marketing campaign example. A Green marketing campaign relies on the ability to reach a large number of targeted respondents in a timely, efficient, and cost-effective manner. The use of telemarketing and mail surveys has been ruled out by the marketing department in this example as being ineffective in the past and there are no resources available to conduct personal interviews with respondents. The IT department has been called to the marketing team meetings to offer input and options that would allow the few marketing team members available to perform this task with great efficiency and effectiveness. The IT department was able to formulate these options after learning that the marketing team had many of the targeted respondents' e-mail addresses, names of social networking Web sites (i.e., LinkedIn, Facebook, etc.) they frequently visit, online magazines and journals they subscribe to, as well as professional associations they belong to:

- Create an online survey, questionnaire, and feedback Web site for the marketing campaign that can be linked from the organization's Internet site and external sites.
- Purchase advertising space on a social networking, professional magazine/journal, and/or professional association Web site.
- Link advertisements back to the organization's marketing campaign Web site to redirect respondents when they click on the ad.
- Place entries in the social network groups that relate to this marketing campaign as a forum and conduit to inform respondents and offer a Web site link back to marketing campaign Web site.
- Send e-mails via IT e-mail server assets directly to target respondents and offer Web site links back to marketing campaign Web site.
- Create a marketing campaign collaborative Web site that allows for searching and indexing of a centrally stored repository of shared documents, notes, and project schedules that the team can upload and retrieve to collaborate among themselves.
- Create a searchable marketing information repository database on IT database systems.
- Create a marketing campaign data mining model from the repository database and other sources of information that will allow the marketing team to run predictions on data using different data mining algorithms on IT business intelligence systems.
- Create a marketing campaign scorecard on IT business intelligence systems that tracks key performance indicators and their associated values, trends, and statuses.

- Create online reports on IT reporting systems that are accessible by internal marketing team members via the intranet and by external sales force personnel via the Internet or extranet that will aid in quicker analysis and decision processing.
- Create marketing campaign work-flow processes via IT-enabled business systems to streamline and integrate work flows.

It is not unheard of for marketing team members to say that their individual and marketing-campaign related performance increased tenfold by having IT-related technology at their disposal. With these types of performance gains perceived, the marketing team can project that this type of IT implementation could be used in future marketing campaigns with the same and even greater level of performance results.

Let's look at performance in an analytical manner via a formula that can offer insight into these perceived performance increases:

$$\text{Performance} = \text{Declarative Knowledge} + \text{Procedural Knowledge} + \text{Motivation}^{14}$$

Declarative knowledge is related to facts, principles, and goals. The marketing team had productive and effective accessibility and data visualization of three sets of information via the marketing Internet portal and the marketing campaign data set that was accumulated during the surveys of targeted respondents. Furthermore, the facts, principles, and goals of the marketing campaign were collaboratively shared and discussed through team meetings, the collaborative portal, and the business intelligence and reporting systems.

Procedural knowledge is based on what is required to perform a task and how to perform that task effectively. This marketing campaign example has been created with a low level of detail in respect to tasks, resource assignment, and integration of IT resources and offerings. This is denoted in the project schedule, process flow charts, procedural documentation, and much more that is viewable on the collaborative portal Web site. Additionally, marketing team members have access to IT collaborative tools, such as NetMeeting, LiveMeeting, and instant messaging through the organization's mail systems; these tools allow team members to gain interactive information on a task or process while actively performing it.

Motivation is the will and ability to focus behavior in a way that increases performance by expending additional effort on work tasks. This can be related to having motivation positively influence the overall good of the organization's environmentally sustainable efforts. Motivation can come from within the self and projected outward with little or no stimulus, or motivation can be stimulated.

Social Responsibility

In the past, the corporate world turned a cold shoulder to being environmentally responsible, citing the fiduciary responsibility to stockholder profits as their main concern. These sentiments reflected a perceived contradiction between corporate objectives and corporate social responsibility (CSR). CSR refers to operating a business in a manner that considers the social and environmental impact created by the business. CSR means a commitment to developing policies that integrate responsible practices into daily business operations and to reporting on progress made toward implementing these practices and adopting operating policies that exceed mere compliance with social and environmental laws. Emphasis on social environmental and economic sustainability has become a focus of many CSR efforts. Aspects of this emphasis and efforts are shown in Figure 3.7.

Socially responsible shareholders have been a key catalyst in asking companies to develop a CSR agenda for environmental sustainability. "Some see this work as charity, philanthropy, or an allocation of

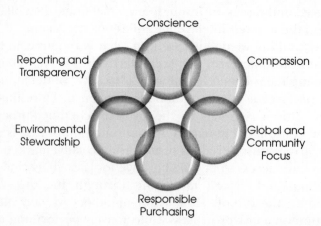

Figure 3.7   Social Responsibility and Environmental Sustainability

resources that could better be donated by shareowners themselves," writes Debra Dunn, Hewlett Packard Senior Vice President for Global Citizenship in the company's 2005 report. "But to us, it is a vital investment in our future, essential to our top-line and bottom-line business success." Corporate social responsibility can contribute to building a stronger brand in two ways. From a capital markets perspective, many analysts and investors believe that a company's brand can be a key growth driver and that firms with a commitment to global citizenship may have advantages in that regard. From a consumer perspective, research suggests that social responsibility is a primary way in which the public forms impressions of companies.[15]

> The United Nations Environment Programme (UNEP) Division of Technology, Industry, and Economics works closely with partners from business and industry to advance their mission and activities in the field of technology, industry, and economics. This involves working with representatives of businesses, large and small, from all parts of the world. It also involves working with related stakeholders, ranging from labor and consumers to NGOs and research organisations.
>
> Our activities in this field include stakeholder dialogue, sharing emerging best practices, developing and promoting materials to build the capacities of managers and employees, inspiring partnership innovation and improving understanding of key corporate responsibility issues on the global sustainable development agenda.
>
> [In o]ur work in the [area] of corporate social responsibility (CSR) or corporate environmental and social responsibility (CESR), as it is also called in UNEP, we underline the environmental pillar in the triple bottom line approach and use environment as entry point when addressing broader sustainability issues. We view corporate citizenship or CSR as a values-based way of conducting business in a manner that advances sustainable development. It seeks positive impact between business operations and society, aware of the close interrelation between business and society. It also shows an awareness that companies, like citizens, have basic rights and duties wherever they operate.[16]

Organizations should strive to get their CSR message and initiatives out to customers and other stakeholders via IT offerings.

One such method is via a CSR Internet portal, such as CSRwire. com, which is a leading source of CSR and sustainability news, reports, events, and information. Members are interested in communicating their corporate citizenship, sustainability, and socially responsible initiatives to a global audience.[17]

> During 2010 and 2011, 89% of companies in the United States and 62% in Europe plan to use IT systems to manage their CSR initiatives, according to a new AMR Research survey. . . . The challenge is often that these systems can help collect historical data, but they aren't very good at helping companies be proactive, monitoring changes in real-time, and helping operatives reduce poor decisions that create more waste of environmental impact. Enterprise-wide visibility and complex proactive control requires enterprise-level information systems. Dashboards and portal systems are likely to provide the answer. 43% of the respondents say a CSR dashboard would be very useful; 29% saying it is critical.[18]

Additionally, an organization's CSR strategy and effort can be assisted with the affiliation and assistance from specialized entities, such as the World Environment Center (WEC), which is "an independent, global non-profit, non-advocacy organization that advances sustainable development through the business practices of member companies and in partnership with governments, multi-lateral organizations, non-governmental organizations, universities, and other stakeholders."[19] The WEC offers the Gold Medal Award as

> one of the most prestigious ways of recognizing a global company's ongoing commitment to the practice of sustainable development. Only global manufacturing, processing, or service corporations that can document well implemented, outstanding, and sustained success are eligible to compete for the award. A potential applicant company must demonstrate global vision and a commitment to sustainable development through innovative application of policies, and international economic, environmental, and social responsibilities.

In 2009, the recipient of the WEC Gold Medal was the Coca-Cola Company and in 2010 Wal-Mart Stores received the Center Gold

Medal for International Corporate Achievement in Sustainable Development.[20]

Regulatory or Voluntarily Compliance

Government regulations with respect to environmental sustainability will increase and become more mainstream throughout the first part of the twenty-first century. This will put pressure on organizations to review on how they will implement compliance, either voluntarily or mandatory.

> The U.S. Environmental Protection Agency (EPA) and state environmental agencies regulate the impact of businesses on the environment. The EPA develops and enforces regulations that implement environmental laws enacted by Congress. Likewise, state agencies enforce regulations that implement laws enacted by the state legislature.
>
> There are dozens of environmental regulations that apply to businesses. The EPA and other agencies help small businesses understand their specific requirements by publishing plain-language guides that explain actions business owners must take to comply with federal regulations. Similarly, most state governments provide similar guidance for laws enforced by state environmental agencies.[21]
>
> The UNEP is the designated authority of the United Nations system in environmental issues at the global and regional level. Its mandate is to coordinate the development of environmental policy consensus by keeping the global environment under review and bringing emerging issues to the attention of governments and the international community for action.[22]
>
> The Green Economy Initiative (GEI) is designed to assist governments in "greening" their economies by reshaping and refocusing policies, investments, and spending towards a range of sectors, such as clean technologies, renewable energies, water services, green transportation, waste management, green buildings, and sustainable agriculture and forests.[23]

Compliance by organizations can be voluntary or mandated. It can be from governmental laws, consumer demands, employee demands, competition, and so on. Voluntary compliance is seen as an alternative to imposed regulations on a company's behavior. Proponents of voluntary compliance argue that it is in a company's own interest to behave socially responsibly and that in pursuit of good public image, the company will cease doing things that could damage its perception by public. Thus, the need for imposing regulatory compliance may diminish.

Now the tide is changing, and there are examples of both industry and government initiatives that aggressively protect the environment. Increasingly, environmental protection is viewed as good business, if not a corporate responsibility, and firms are introducing proactive measures instead of simply reacting to government mandates.

Organizations should be conscious of Green consumers and environmental watchdog groups who are strong advocates and participants of environmental sustainability movements and legislation, review organizational compliance, and Greenwashing tactics. It is not only important what actions an organization takes relating to compliance efforts, but how they are perceived by customers, investors, partners, and vendors.

IT resources and offerings in the past have assisted with organizational compliance efforts related to the Health Insurance Portability and Accountability Act, the Sarbanes-Oxley Act, Securities and Exchange Commission rules, and the like. This would also be the case for Kyoto Protocol compliance by having IT offering systems that can achieve high performance, reliable, efficient management of documents and data, along with electronic reporting of carbon footprint and greenhouse gas emissions, and so on.

Partnerships and Alliances

This part of the strategy framework states that organizations should pursue assistance with their environmental sustainability goal and Green initiatives to benefit from others' experiences, knowledge sharing, collaboration, and exposure to new technologies, consulting services, and much more. Many organizations have embarked on the goal of environmental sustainability and have completed many Green initiatives. There is no reason to reinvent the wheel or go down the road of pursuing environmental sustainability alone. Partnerships and alliances can be formed with governments and with private and nonprofit organizations.

U.S. Environmental Protection Agency   According to the EPA: "EPA Partnership Programs address a wide variety of environmental issues by working collaboratively with companies, organizations, communities, and individuals. There are now more than 13,000 firms and other organizations participating in EPA Partnership Programs." The link to the EPA partnership programs is: www.epa .gov/partners/programs/index.htm

European Environmental Agency

The European Environment Agency (EEA) is an agency of the European Union. Our task is to provide sound, independent information on the environment. We are a major information source for those involved in developing, adopting, implementing and evaluating environmental policy, and also the general public. Currently, the EEA has 32 member countries. The regulation establishing the EEA was adopted by the European Union in 1990. It came into force in late 1993 immediately after the decision was taken to locate the EEA in Copenhagen. Work started in earnest in 1994. The regulation also established the European environment information and observation network (Eionet). EEA's mandate is:

- To help the Community and member countries make informed decisions about improving the environment, integrating environmental considerations into economic policies and moving towards sustainability
- To coordinate the European environment information and observation network[24]

Eco-Friendly Organizations   Corporations that form partnerships with eco-friendly organizations can add credibility to their Green initiative efforts and show Green consumers their commitment to addressing environmental challenges. A few eco-friendly organizations are:

- EarthFirst!
- Environmental Defense Fund
- Greenpeace
- National Audubon Society
- National Resources Defense Council
- National Wildlife Federation
- Rainforest Action Network
- Sierra Club
- World Wildlife Fund

Green Technology Alliance

The Green Technology Alliance (GTA) focuses on creating the infrastructure, venues, support, and knowledge base to accelerate the adoption of both existing and emerging Green technologies by working to accomplish four interrelated goals:

1. Showcase and develop the green technologies of today and tomorrow.
2. Create the strategies required to deploy real solutions that deliver an immediate business benefit to the companies that invest in Green Technologies; such as reduced costs, improved efficiency, and greater productivity.
3. Enable and accelerate the adoption of new technologies to create jobs and promote economic development in both the public and private sector.
4. Develop a reproducible sustainable economies model (the STSE model) based on the principles of a true alliance that not only supports our economy and planet but sustains it.

The founding organizations of the GTA believe that an alliance is required to create value exchanges that support sustainable development. *Remember green must equal green first* . . . meaning it must have an identifiable business benefit for long-term value and adoption—especially when change is involved.[25]

Integrating IT into Strategy

The concept of integrating IT department resources and offerings into the Green strategy framework is via the many examples that were mentioned in each of the strategy's other framework components, but is also a dedicated important strategy framework component (see Figure 3.3). What this component of the strategy framework shows is the need to strategically review the integration of the IT department in each Green initiative to be implemented as part of the organization's overall effort to achieve its environmental sustainability goal. Remember: Your competitors are integrating their IT departments into their Green initiatives. Don't let them outstrategize you.

Green initiatives can range from utilizing IT department data center resources to reducing the organization's overall energy consumption, greener desktops, deploying Environmental

Management System applications and architecture, and using external customer-facing Web sites to report environmental sustainability and the organization's socially responsible actions.

The IT department can assist in the deployment of an EMS, via the IT resources and offerings, to allow for the EMS to be able to effectively manage and reduce an organization's impact on the environment, improve operational efficiency, identify opportunities for cost saving, and reduce environmental liability. The IT department will be involved with discussions and implementation of the application and server architecture to host the EMS within the business.

The IT department must be integrated into the organization's Green initiatives from the very top, with the CEO and CIO. This integration is further sustained and built on through the organization with the aid of the project management office, which ensures that each Green initiative project is not funded or approved without IT department integration.

Summary

This chapter offered strategy concepts, tools, and a framework that organizations that are beginning or modifying their Green initiative efforts can use. The strategy framework offered examples, justifications, and benefits on how the IT department resources and offerings are of great value to many organizational Green initiative efforts when they are integrated with cohesiveness, effectiveness, and maximization. The integration can result in IT-enabled business programs that can benefit from the strategic IT-Business relationship.

The Green initiative strategy with IT departments can benefit from the utilization of strategy mapping and relationships with outside environmental organizations, government agencies, government programs, partnerships, and much more. Additionally, the need to solidify and agree on a well-defined strategy is essential to the success of Green initiatives and to achieve the overall goal of environmental sustainability.

Notes

1. www.environmentalleader.com/2008/11/11/lack-of-executive-sponsorship-accountability-hurt-green-programs/
2. www.ccnl.ca/greenerfutures/pdf/building-a-green-business-culture.pdf

3. F. John Reh, "Company Culture: What It Is and How to Change It," About.com Guide, http://management.about.com/cs/generalmanagement/a/company-culture.htm
4. www.gdrc.org/sustbiz/green/doc-cons_vitalsigns.html
5. WorldWatch Institute, "Transforming Cultures," http://blogs.worldwatch.org/transformingcultures/
6. M. Brower and W. Leon, *The Consumer's Guide to Effective Environmental Choices* (New York: Three Rivers Press, 2009).
7. D. Dunphy, A. Griffiths, and S. Benn, *Organizational Change for Corporate Sustainability* (New York: Routledge, 2003).
8. www.johnson.cornell.edu/sge/
9. www.environmentalleader.com/2007/08/03/hsbc-names-head-of-new-climate-change-center-of-excellence/
10. www.unm.edu/~rattner/picmet97.pdf
11. United States General Accounting Office, Accounting and Information Management Division, "Business Process Reengineering Assessment Guide" May 1997, GAO/AIMD-10.1.15.
12. Thomas H. Davenport, "Will Participative Makeovers of Business Processes Succeed Where Reengineering Failed?" *Planning Review* (January 1995): 24.
13. Jerry Harbour, "Integrated Performance Management: A Conceptual, System-Based Model," *ISPI* 48, no. 7 (August 2009): 10–14.
14. H. Aguinis, *Performance Management* (Upper Saddle River, NJ: Prentice Hall, 2007).
15. www.hp.com/hpinfo/globalcitizenship/07gcreport/pdf/hp2005gcreport.pdf?jumpid=reg_R1002_USEN
16. www.unep.fr/scp/business/index.htm
17. www.csrwire.com/
18. www.amresearch.com/content/view.aspx?compURI=tcm:7-19381&title=U.S.+Companies+Lead+Europe+in+Corporate+Social+Responsibility+Data+Integration++
19. www.wec.org/
20. www.csrwire.com/press/press_release/28312-Walmart-Stores-to-Receive-2010-World-Environment-Center-Gold-Medal-for-International-Corporate-Achievement-in-Sustainable-Development
21. www.business.gov/business-law/environmental-regulations/
22. www.unep.org/resources/gov/
23. www.unep.ch/etb/publications/Green Economy/G 20 policy brief FINAL.pdf
24. www.eea.europa.eu/about-us/who
25. www.greentechnologyalliance.org/gta/about/

CHAPTER 4

Green Initiative Planning with IT

This chapter offers in-depth information on planning concepts and processes that can be utilized to integrate the information technology (IT) department into the overall environmental sustainability goal in an effective and productive manner. The Green initiative planning stage has the goal of achieving environmental sustainability for the organization by incorporating a dynamic, long-term strategy that is of strategic business value, has processes and flow, and has flexibility. With the use of the environmental management system (EMS) and a planning process framework, the planning stage integrates the IT department's resources and offerings into Green initiative efforts in a way that will substantially benefit the planning stage and processes.

Planning Stage Overview

What does a business want from its Green initiatives and from its IT department to reach its environmental sustainability goals? The end game is to achieve the strategic goal of environmental sustainability with Green initiatives being implemented to achieve the goal. Assistance from the IT department will be used to complement the Green initiative efforts. Thus, the IT department will need to have offerings that are reliable, compliant, and cost effective and that adapt to the ever-changing needs of the business.

The planning stage is where business and the IT department work as partners to determine how IT resources and offerings will be focused to deliver productive results for Green initiatives to succeed. Doing this requires:

- Understanding the business strategy and requirements and how the current IT services support the business
- Understanding what IT productivity and reliability means to this organization and how it will be measured and improved by reviewing and taking action where needed
- Understanding what business- and IT-specific policy require-ments exist and how they impact the Green initiative plan-ning process
- Providing the financial structure and executive sponsorship to support the business and IT integration to drive the right decisions

Green initiative planning with the IT department provides value to the organization's environmental sustainability goal by making decisions to utilize those IT offerings that assist Green initiatives in their completion and effectiveness as well as the overall sustainabil-ity strategy. This value will be denoted in each component of the plan and throughout the planning stage.

Why is the IT department so able to align effectively with Green initiatives efforts? It comes down to the simple fact that the IT department's mission should be to strategically align to an organization's objectives, policies, and procedures in a cohesive approach to deliver the desired set of offerings and resources that support the business strategy. The IT department completes this mis-sion by consistently managing quality, costs, and reliability to achieve the organization's desired outcomes. During the planning stage, the IT department resources work with the business to align business objectives and functions with IT department's capabilities and con-straints. Thus, the IT department uses these alignment processes and guidelines to serve as a road map for future departmental funding, structuring, and offerings. IT must continually evolve and strive to adapt to an organization's ever-changing needs, one of which is to achieve environmental sustainability. This is what makes the IT department strategically valuable to an organization.

The planning stage is a culmination of many different business concepts, (i.e., the environmental sustainability goal and the inte-gration of IT). Figure 4.1 offers insight into a formula that helps visualize the IT department integration aspect along with the

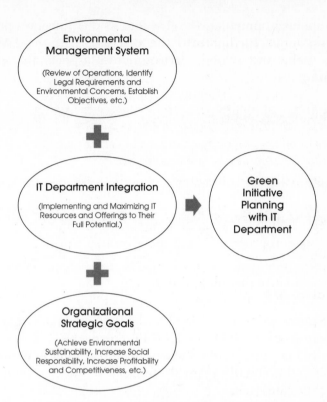

Figure 4.1 Formula for Green Initiative Planning with IT

interrelationship of the EMS and organizational strategic goals as they culminate in assisting with an organization's Green initiative planning effort.

> Environmental Management System + IT Department
> Integration + Organizational Strategic Goals
> = Green Initiative Planning with IT Department

The EMS is essential to the planning stage in many respects, which will be discussed throughout the chapter. Discussion of the planning process flow provides insight into each step of the plan.

Environmental Management System

An EMS is a set of management tools and principles designed to create the administrative procedures that a company needs to integrate environmental concerns into its daily business practices. Before we move further into the discussion of the EMS, two terms must be understood: environmental aspects and environmental impacts.

Environmental Aspect

Element of an activity, product, or service of a company that is causing or can cause an environmental impact.

Environmental Impact

Actual interaction with or impact on the environment.

ISO Standard: EMS

The EMS developed and outlined by the International Organization for Standardization (ISO) in ISO14001 provides a widely recognized set of principles and standards for integrating environmental management into quality control and other business activities.

The ISO states that:

> An EMS meeting the requirements of ISO 14001:2004 is a management tool enabling an organization of any size or type to:
> - identify and control the environmental impact of its activities, products or services, and to
> - improve its environmental performance continually, and to
> - implement a systematic approach to setting environmental objectives and targets, to achieving these and to demonstrating that they have been achieved.[1]

The EMS offers a continuous improvement cycle, as shown in Figure 4.2. In its planning component, organizations conduct reviews of operations, identify legal requirements and environmental concerns, establish objectives, evaluate alternatives, set targets, and devise a plan for meeting those targets.

Whether building your EMS from preexisting systems, starting a brand-new EMS system, or purchasing one from a vendor, potential benefits of an EMS that is based on ISO 14001 include:

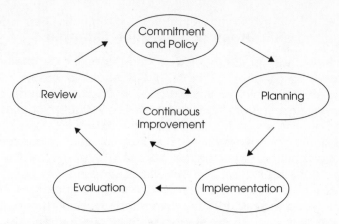

Figure 4.2   EMS Continuous Improvement Cycle

Source: United States Environmental Protection Agency, "Environmental Management Systems—A Design for the Environment Approach," 2009. Retrieved December 12, 2009, from the EPA Web site: www.epa.gov/dfe/pubs/iems/bulletins/bullet01/whatems.html

- Improvements in overall environmental performance and compliance
- Increased efficiency and potential cost savings when managing environmental obligations
- Predictability and consistency in managing environmental obligations
- More effective targeting of scarce environmental management resources
- Enhanced public posture with outside stakeholders

Organizations may wonder whether their existing environmental-related activities, processes, and/or systems can be integrated into the EMS under ISO 14001. The answer is yes. The standard is flexible and does not require organizations to retool their existing activities. The standard establishes a management framework by which organizations can systematically identify and reduce their impact on the environment. For example, many organizations, including counties and municipalities, have active and effective pollution prevention activities under way. These could be incorporated into the overall EMS under ISO 14001. One such system that can benefit by integration into the EMS under 14001 are Environmental Information Management Systems (EIMS).

EMS: Green Organization Example

Intel maintains a company-wide certification to the internationally recognized ISO 14001:2004 standard to ensure Intel manufacturing sites maintain a comprehensive environmental management system that clearly defines and tracks global performance to environmental goals and initiatives. All Intel Wafer Fabrication and Assembly Test sites that manufacture commercial product are registered to the ISO 14001:2004 standard by a third-party registrar under a multi-site registration.

As Intel continues to expand manufacturing operations into new global markets, they are committed to their philosophy for implementing world class environmental programs and certifying new manufacturing sites to the ISO 14001:2004 standard. Intel has maintained a multi-site ISO14001:2004 certification for all manufacturing locations since 2001 and will continue to demonstrate its internationally recognized commitment to worldwide environmental excellence by completing independent third-party audits at various sites each year.

New sites implement an ISO 14001:2004 based environmental management system at their start up and are registered as soon as enough time has passed to gather historical data. Sites must demonstrate that their environmental management system has been in use for a minimum of six months prior to registration.

Source: www.intel.com/intel/other/ehs/iso.htm

EMS: Green Software Example

The Intelex Environmental Management System provides a framework for organizations to improve their environmental performance by incorporating environmental considerations into their business decisions and risk management efforts. The system also enables organizations to define and enforce corporate-wide environmental policies, identify environmental aspects, maintain regulatory compliance, and demonstrate due diligence. Intelex's Environmental Management System enables compliance with government legislation and industry standards such as

ISO 14001, RC14001, and OHSAS 18001. To facilitate compliance, Intelex's EMS includes the Intelex Compliance Management Suite, which consists of Legal Requirements Management; Permits & Related Activities; Emergency Response; Maintenance, Measurement & Monitoring, and Operational Control modules. For organizations preparing to become ISO 14001 registered, the Intelex Environmental Management System can also come pre-loaded with an ISO 14001 Implementation Project Plan. Intelex's software will generate a custom implementation schedule based on the start date and target completion date determined by your organization's ISO 14001 Implementation Team. The system's built-in reporting functionality will allow end users to create printable, real-time progress reports for a visual representation of tasks completed.

Source: www.intelex.com/Environmental_Management-150-1product.aspx

Environmental Information Management System

An EIMS is used to store, manage, verify, protect, retrieve, and archive organizational environmental data. The EIMS stores operational and historical data in a database and a Geographic Information System (GIS) that will allow for detailed and aggregated data analysis and reporting to the organizational stakeholders in a timely manner with the highest level of data quality. Environmental data that is available within an EIMS can be of many types and from different sources. Some examples include:

- Employee health and safety
- Environmental incidents
- Regulatory and compliance
- Chemical inventory tracking
- Environmental impacts

The EIMS database can be used by applications available to users to query, display, export, and print data. Additionally, typically there are several data management utilities available and the ability to perform mapping/GIS functions. The GIS data contains geospatial information about environmental surveillance, compliance, and remediation efforts. The GIS services typically include paper maps and Web applications for interactive spatial queries and mapping.

Contact your IT department to locate an EIMS or similar database storage system within your organization. The IT department can assist you by querying the application portfolio listing that contains a listing of enterprise-related applications.

Planning Stage Process Flow

Now that we have discussed an overview of the planning stage and the use and importance of an EMS during this stage, it is time to dive deeper into the plan's process flow. It is here where we will also show how the IT department contributes and factors into the planning stage. The IT department's contribution can be in the utilization of its technical and human resources, systems, databases, networks, and much more. IT technical resources can also be viewed as a factor in evaluating environmental aspects and impacts. One such example is with the cooling and energy consumption of IT data centers. These data centers can use large amounts of electricity and create a large carbon footprint when not designed and implemented in an eco-friendly manner.

The processes, which are shown in Figure 4.3, are to be implemented in a serial manner, but they should allow for feedback, and overall collaboration among participating organizational personnel and entities.

Steering Committee

A group of high-level stakeholders who are responsible for providing guidance on the environmental sustainability goal of the organization will be formed to determine the required Green initiatives and efforts necessary to fulfill the goal. Do not confuse this steering committee with executive sponsors; rather they are an extension of executive sponsors. The steering committee will assist in spreading and managing the strategic objective of environmental sustainability throughout a much larger and deeper portion of the organization as well as reaching out externally to customers. The steering committee is to be formed as a leadership body of committed and organizationally representative individuals who will carry out the duties stated in the committee's mission statement which contains the committee guiding principles, membership role definitions and authority, and much more.

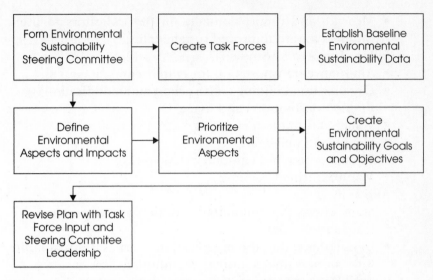

Figure 4.3   Planning Stage Process Flow with IT Department

Examples of components, tasks, and processes of a steering committee operating and guiding framework are listed next.

- Mission Statement
- Committee Web Portal
  - Collaborative portal
  - Contains mission statement
  - Membership listing
  - Meeting dates and notes from prior meetings
  - Objectives and goals
- Committee Guiding Principles
  - Identify and establish sustainable objectives and goals.
  - Provide a framework for developing sustainable procedures and initiatives.
  - Communicate awareness to all stakeholders.
  - Involve, engage, and collaborate with all stakeholders.
  - Develop an organization-wide culture of sustainability.
  - Educate for sustainable community participation.
  - Respond to concerns raised by stakeholders.
  - Conduct all initiatives in a transparent and sustainable manner.

- Measure and report annually on the indicators to track progress toward improved sustainability.
- Pillars: Issues to Be Studied
  - Alternative transportation for employees
  - Organization building construction and modifications
  - Energy consumption and usage
  - Water consumption and usage
  - Health and well-being
  - IT data center and equipment Greening
  - Manufacturing Greening
- Authority
  - State where the committee's authority and power come from and through.
  - Define this within the organization chart as a virtual entity with connections to sources of authority.
- Overall Desired Outcomes
  - Achieve environmental sustainability for the organization.
  - Improve the quality of the natural environment around an organization's facilities.
  - Decrease the organization's carbon footprint and negative impact on the environment.
  - Achieve economic benefits from establishing of environmental sustainability and eco-friendly practices.
- Membership and Terms of Membership
  - Permanent and contributing standing members could be from the these areas of the organization and external entities:
    - IT department
    - Environmental sustainability department
    - Building and facilities operations
    - Manufacturing
    - Logistics
    - Product services and support
    - Customer representatives
  - Ad hoc nonstanding and casual participating members who can offer substantial value to steering committees efforts
- Accountability
  - List to whom the sustainability steering committee reports directly and indirectly.
- Meeting Types, Frequency, Location, Method

Task Forces

An Environmental Sustainability Task Force (ESTF) is created to assist a steering committee in formulating, modifying, and solidifying the plan. ESTFs are formed during the planning stage and are implemented throughout the life of the overall environmental sustainability effort. They are related to the Green initiatives the organization will be implementing to accomplish its overall goal of environmental sustainability.

An ESTF can be used as an exploratory, task-oriented, research-based, or fact-finding tool to substantiate, negate, validate, or hypothesize Green initiative concepts. An ESTF is a way for the steering committee to get out into the organization, with customers, and with Green-related partners and associations, to strengthen, reinforce, and enrich the planning stage.

Types of ESTFs that are created to assist the steering committee include:

- Environmental sustainability organization impact analysis
- Baseline environmental data gathering
- Green initiative value chain analysis
- Environmental regulatory compliance
- Training and awareness
- IT integration and IT Greening benefits
- Performance assessment
- Auditing and reporting
- Social responsibility enrichment analysis
- Sustainable technology availability and purchasing

Components, tasks, and processes of an ESTF operating and guidance framework include:

- Mission statement
- Link within steering committee Web portal for ESTF-specific information and collaborative efforts
- Members
- Goals
- Meeting schedule, types, and notes
- Work groups within ESTF that will be assigned particular tasks and offer support in specific areas of expertise
- Report and feedback to steering committee

Baseline Environmental Sustainability Data

Before environmental aspects and impacts can be determined and before environmental impacts can be prioritized, an organization needs to perform a environmental baseline data analysis. This analysis will establish the foundation of data related to environmental sustainability, regulatory compliance, and the like that reflects the organization's current environmental sustainability state. An outline of a baseline environmental sustainability data analysis operating and procedural framework is shown next.

- Assessed Areas for Environmental Baseline Data
  - Water consumption and usage
  - Hazardous materials and waste usage and creation
  - Regulatory compliance permits, levels, and participation rates
  - Transportation methods and types of employees and supply chain
  - Levels of usage of videoconferencing versus employee travel for meetings
  - Power consumption and usage (emphasizing IT data centers and desktops)
  - Alternative energy usage levels
  - Emissions levels
  - Carbon footprint levels
  - Building and construction eco-friendly levels and practices
- Informational and Data Sources
  - Organizational Environmental Information Management System
  - Regulation and compliance: both internal and government related, environmental inspection results, etc.
  - Physical site locations and visits: visual, equipment readings, etc.
  - Prior environmental assessments
  - Building and facility blueprints and/or plans
  - Organizational and department-level points of contacts (i.e., subject matter experts)
- Tasks and Processes (see Figure 4.4)
  - Collect all applicable data from source systems, document repositories, and so on. Collection process may entail the creation of queries from database systems, custom and ad hoc reports, data extracts, movement of data via

an extract-transform-load (ETL) process, and document text searches. The interaction with the IT department can be of great value during this process to gain access to data sources and assistance with the ETL process.

- Collaborate with the steering committee and other personnel to discuss the data and determine if additional data is required to complete the environmental analysis.
- Identify gaps within the data collection process that will hamper the environmental analysis. Perform collaborative risk analysis of continuing baseline environmental assessment (EA) with gaps.
- Analyze the environmental baseline data collected via a predefined analysis process. Create baseline key performance indicators (KPIs) from baseline data and aggregated reports for comparison with later data. Analysis will identify and relate current issues associated with attaining environmental sustainability.

Figure 4.4 offers a graphical representation of the task and processes to assist with defining, collecting, and structuring data within the EA data assessment.

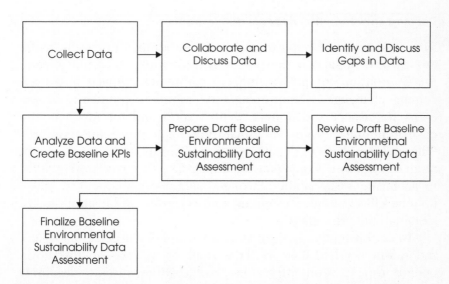

Figure 4.4   Baseline Environmental Sustainability Data Assessment Tasks

Discuss the availability of dashboard and scorecard software with your IT department. The use of a business performance management (BPM) software package can greatly assist with the creation of dashboards, scorecards, reports, and KPIs to display the organization's environmental baseline data. To benefit from the BPM software package, follow these recommendations to establish a baseline environmental sustainability data assessment that will reference baseline data:

- Prepare a draft baseline environmental sustainability data assessment that is consistent with a standard within your organization, government environmental agency, or international standard that will document the outcome of your environmental analysis.
- Review the draft baseline assessment with the steering committee. Determine edits, possible additional appendixes, and ambiguous analysis that needs further clarification. Make necessary changes and review again until review process is complete.
- Finalize the baseline environmental sustainability data assessment via official approval process. Make the draft assessment available on steering committee Web portal for those involved to review and refer to.

Defining Environmental Aspects and Impacts

The need to relate departments and operations to environmental aspects and impacts is the part of the planning stage that creates the foundation for prioritizing environmental impacts and overcoming challenges. Department and operation granularity is necessary for aspect and impact identification and for much of the environmental sustainability planning and coordination efforts. One such emphasis of departmental granularity is with local government operations. "Coordination among City departments is critical to achieving sustainability. Stronger alignment among City stakeholders will streamline resources, spur creativity, and institutionalize sustainability principles."[2]

To establish an organization's environmental aspects, an organization will need to answer: "How does or will the organization's operations (i.e., products, services, and activities) interact negatively or positively with the environment now (actual) or in the future (potential)?" Not all environmental aspects cause environmental impacts in their current state. However, they offer the potential for an impact. For example, storage of a chemical solvent is an environmental aspect. But if the container does not leak, there is no immediate or actual impact on the environment from such storage. A future leak would indicate a potential future impact. Additional considerations when determining aspects are:

- Ensure EMS is utilized.
- Refer to baseline data EA for aid in aspect and impact analysis.
- Determine core operations and supporting activities based on both products and services where applicable.
- Construct input/process/output diagrams that have environmental relevance utilizing process mapping software (i.e., disposal of chemicals, use of recyclable material in production, etc.) within defined processes.
- Identify environmental aspects and impacts from process maps. Additional concepts that can assist with this are as follows:
  - Should have influence and be controllable (consumption of electricity) by the organization. Thus, do not select aspects that are outside the control (electrical generation) of the organization.
  - Can be positive or negative on the environment.
  - Should encompass onsite (manufacturing) and offsite (servicing equipment) organizational operations. Offsite could also refer to offshoring and outsourcing.
- Develop a list or matrix of environmental aspects and impacts.
- Prioritize environmental aspects based on approved criteria and processes.

Process Mapping One tool to relate operation and activities to environmental aspects is process mapping. Ask the IT department for software availability to aid in the creation of the process maps. Process mapping can be in the form of flow charts, business process models, and the like. Choose a software package that allows for collaboration, allows you to implement a standard, offers ease of use and clarity, and is offered and supported by your IT department. Thus, ensure that your IT department is in the loop and consulted about software application.

Process Mapping

According to the EPA, process mapping is "an approach to systematically analyze a particular process. It involves mapping each individual step, or unit operation, undertaken in that process in chronological sequence. Once individual steps are identified, they can be analyzed in more detail. For example, the environmental aspects of a given step can be identified by analyzing its inputs and outputs."

Source: ww.epa.gov/dfe/pubs/iems/tools/process.pdf

Identifying Environmental Aspects Identify the environmental aspects within your organization that are applicable to the overall goal of environmental sustainability, can result in an environmental impact, and can be influenced and be controlled by your organization. This will create a respectable amount of environmental aspect/impact combinations that can be prioritized into Green initiative efforts as short-term and long-term goals with objectives. Some questions that can be asked to assist in the identification process are listed next.

- Has any prior environmental aspect and impact analysis been initiated anywhere within the organization?
- Which operations and activities, both internal and external, interact with the environment in a way that has resulted or will result in an impact?
- What types of natural resources are used in the organization's manufacturing and production processes and are being shipped outside the organization?
- Rather than just looking for regulatory compliance and regulations, what types of fuels and energy sources are being used?
- What current environmental permits, regulatory controls, and standards is the organization adhering to, planning to adhere to in the future, or have obtained?
- What types of wastes are generated (i.e., e-waste from computer and IT-related equipment, chemical, etc.)?
- Do your buildings and facilities implement eco-friendly, renewable energy (solar panels), energy-efficient equipment and practices?

- Does your organization create emissions (via your service delivery truck fleet, smokestacks, etc.) in the air or water?
- What is the geographic scope of the impact (i.e., local, regional, national, and global, etc.)?
- What is the typical frequency and duration of the aspect?

For those organizations that operate globally, regionally, or nationally, the answers to these questions will be more complex than for organizations that operate locally only. Nevertheless, those organizations that operate beyond the local community should consider their impact everywhere their operations and activities impact on. To move production and manufacturing operations from one country to another does not relieve an organization of the need to identify environmental aspects/impacts in the new location. Operating globally requires acting responsible, ethical, and socially responsible globally.

Many different and similar organizational operations and activities have environmental aspects. Having a way to categorize them offers the organization a way to group and evaluate them. Categories of aspects that could be used to assist in this task include:

- Pollution: air, land, water
- Recycling
- Waste creation
- Greenhouse gases: global warming
- Toxic contamination
- Energy use: renewable
- Energy use: nonrenewable
- Energy usage waste
- Conservation of natural resources

Evaluating Environmental Impacts   Now that the environmental aspects have been identified, it is time to associate the aspect to an environmental impact. The organization must create questions and criteria to map an environmental aspect to an impact and to determine the type, level, and degree of the impact. Some questions that can assist in evaluating of environmental impacts are listed next.

- Does the environmental impact have a current government regulation associated with it?

- Has a previous environmental impact assessment been performed within the organization that can supplement this process?
- What is the geographic scope of the impact (i.e., local, regional, national, global)?
- Which parts of the environment does the impact affect (i.e., air, land, water, soil)?
- Is the impact a current/actual impact on the environment, or is it only a potential impact?
- Does the impact pose a negative (contamination, pollution, etc.) or a positive effect (i.e., conservation, reduction in global warming, etc.) on the environment?
- What is the typical frequency and duration of the impact?
- What is considered to be the degree of the impact on the environment (i.e., severe, mild, modest, low)?
- What significant residual or cascading effects does the environmental impact create?
- Is the impact aligned with the organization's environmental sustainability and ethical and socially responsible practices?
- Is the impact solely caused from within the organization, part of a partnership, a component of a diverse supply chain, and so on?

Environmental Impact Statement Database   A source of environmental impacts is within the EPA's Environmental Impact Statement (EIS) database. The National Environmental Policy Act (NEPA) requires federal agencies to integrate environmental values into their decision-making processes by considering the environmental impacts of their proposed actions and reasonable alternatives to those actions. To meet NEPA requirements, federal agencies prepare a detailed statement known as an EIS. EPA reviews and comments on EISs prepared by those federal agencies, maintains a national filing system for all EISs, and ensures that its own actions comply with NEPA.

Review the EIS database to see how government agencies have defined environmental impacts: www.epa.gov/compliance/nepa/eisdata.html.

Environmental Aspects and Impacts Mapping   With the list of aspects formulated and with environmental impact mapping criteria and guidelines defined, a table mapping environmental aspects to impacts, aspect category, and operation or service activity can be created. An example of such a mapping table is shown in Table 4.1, which presents a small sample of aspects that will be defined in a typical organization.

Table 4.1   Environmental Aspects and Impact Mapping

Operation or Service Activity	Environmental Aspect	Aspect Category	Environmental Impact (Effect)	Actual or Potential Impact
Disposal of IT equipment (desktops, servers, etc.)	E-waste generation	Waste creation	Landfill space usage	Actual
Recycling of IT equipment (desktops, servers, etc.)	E-waste recycling	Recycling	Conservation of landfill space	Actual
IT data center power and cooling	Hydroelectric electricity usage	Energy use: renewable	Greenhouse gas reduction	Actual
Fleet vehicle: delivery	Vehicle air emissions (CO_2)	Greenhouse gases: global warming	Degradation of air quality	Actual
Office/ administrative activities	Recycled paper in printers	Recycling	Conservation of landfill space	Actual
Coffee break rooms	Styrofoam cup use	Waste creation	Landfill space usage	Actual
Chemical manufacturing and shipping	Chemical spills and leaks	Contamination	Soil and water contamination	Actual
Chemical storage handling	Solvent storage	Contamination	Soil and water contamination	Potential

(Continued)

Table 4.1   (Continued)

Operation or Service Activity	Environmental Aspect	Aspect Category	Environmental Impact (Effect)	Actual or Potential Impact
Chemical plant maintenance	Chemical air releases	Greenhouse gases: global warming	Degradation of air quality	Actual
Building heating	Oil fuel burning	Energy use: nonrenewable	Greenhouse gas creation	Actual
Natural gas bus service for campus employees	Vehicle air emissions (CO_2)	Energy use: nonrenewable	Greenhouse gas reductions	Actual

Prioritize Environmental Aspects

Organizations that actively manage their environmental impacts typically have a method for prioritizing them within the EMS. The method selected can vary due to the size of the organization, the amount of environmental aspects and impacts, the amount and importance of the effort in establishing environmental sustainability, and the like. The method can range from simple to very complex analysis, computations, and categorizations; no matter which method is chosen, the goal is to establish the level of significance and determine which aspects and impacts are to be labeled as significant.

Five prioritizing steps that fall between simple and very complex are presented next, thus offering an example that could be used by an organization for comparisons, implementation, and/or training.

Step 1: Choose Criteria for Evaluating Significance   The first step is the establishment of criteria and guidelines for the evaluation of significance. Organizations have different views on common and consistent aspects present within them due to their interpretation of various variables. Thus, no universal and standard criteria and set of guidelines are used across organizations.

Guidelines will help the process by offering clearer and consistent interpretations of the criteria with respect to variables. Removing ambiguity and increasing clarity allows for consistently and effectively prioritizing assignments. The guidelines must prevent the evaluating of very similar environmental aspects that will result in having different criteria. Very similar aspects should have the same criteria as to increase consistent interpretations of aspects.

The criteria an organization finalizes should reflect its economic, social, and environmental values, policies, and strategic goals. An ESTF should contain diverse members throughout your organization to establish the depth and breadth of organizational knowledge and exposure. You can use the next list of criteria for determining significance as a reference and starting point. Modify them to fit your organization's needs.

- Impact on local, regional, national environment
- Impact on global environment (e.g., ozone depletion, climate change)
- High level of severity of impact
- Regulatory compliance, fines, permits
- Impact on operational efficiency
- Impact of overall environmental sustainability strategic goal
- Impact on employee health and safety
- Impact on supply chain
- Impact on customers
- Cost level to resolve impact immediately
- Cost level to resolve impact later (e.g., fines, competitiveness in Green markets, lawsuits)
- Risk level to resolve impact immediately
- Risk level to resolve impact later (e.g., fines, additional environmental impact, legal issues)
- Business value: Green marketing and Green consumer purchasing
- Business value: social responsibility

Step 2: Relate to Organization's Strategic Environmental Sustainability Goal Every environmental aspect and its associated impact should be analyzed against the overall environmental sustainability goal to determine its influence on achieving the goal. Some aspects and their impacts will have a stronger influence, concern, and reaction from the organization to ensure that they are addressed and resolved to keep the overall goal of environmental sustainability achievable within the organization.

Table 4.2   Assessment of Environmental Sustainability Goals

Environmental Aspect	Environmental Impact (Effect)	Related to Environmental Sustainability Goal
E-waste generation	Landfill space usage	Yes
E-waste recycling	Conservation of landfill space	Yes
Hydroelectric electricity usage	Greenhouse gas reduction	Yes
Vehicle air emissions (CO_2)	Degradation of air quality	Yes
Recycled paper in printers	Conservation of landfill space	Yes
Styrofoam cup use	Landfill space usage	Yes
Chemical spills and leaks	Soil and water contamination	Yes
Solvent storage	Soil and water contamination	Yes
Chemical air releases	Degradation of air quality	Yes
Oil fuel burning	Greenhouse gas creation	Yes

This step allows for those involved in the decision-making process to review what is to be called a significant aspect and impact. Furthermore, the step is also a check and type of validation that the planning stage consistently addresses and refers to the strategic environmental sustainability goal of the organization. It could also be a function of an ESTF with an audit- or governance-related task.

Table 4.2 continues the effort shown in Table 4.1 with an additional column for the assignment of a "Yes" or "No" to reflect the aspect's relation to the goal.

Step 3: Evaluate Your Environmental Aspects According to Criteria of Significance   Now that you have determined which criteria for evaluating your environmental aspects are important to your organization, it is time to lay the foundation for determining their level of significance. Table 4.3 shows the result of the example we

Table 4.3   Prioritization and Level of Significance

Environmental Aspect	Environmental Impact (Effect)	Related to Environmental Sustainability Goal	Criteria of Significance
E-waste generation	Landfill Space usage	Yes	Impact on local environment
E-waste recycling	Conservation of landfill space	Yes	Impact on local environment
Hydroelectric electricity usage	Greenhouse gas reduction	Yes	Impact on global environment (e.g., ozone depletion, climate change)
Vehicle air emissions (CO_2)	Degradation of air quality	Yes	Impact of global environment
Recycled paper in printers	Conservation of landfill space	Yes	Impact on natural resources
Styrofoam cup use	Landfill space usage	Yes	Impact on local environment
Chemical spills and leaks	Soil and water contamination	Yes	Impact on local environment
Solvent storage	Soil and water contamination	Yes	Impact on local environment
Chemical air releases	Degradation of air quality	Yes	Impact on global environment
Oil fuel burning	Greenhouse gas creation	Yes	Impact on global environment (e.g., ozone depletion, climate change)

have been using. The table combines the environmental aspect and impact from the previous tables and inputs the criteria of significance that were discussed in step 1.

Step 4: Evaluate Your Environmental Aspects According to Level of Significance   The next step is to evaluate each aspect and its associated impact, environmental sustainability relation, and criteria significance to establish a type of numerical scoring or symbol-related prioritization system. This example, shown in Table 4.4, uses a

Table 4.4 Prioritization and Level of Significance

Environmental Aspect	Environmental Impact (Effect)	Related to Environmental Sustainability Goal	Criteria of Significance	Level of Significance
E-waste generation	Landfill space usage	Yes	Impact on local environment	H
E-waste recycling	Conservation of landfill space	Yes	Impact on local environment	H
Hydroelectric electricity usage	Greenhouse gas reduction	Yes	Impact on global environment (e.g., ozone depletion, climate change)	M
Vehicle air emissions (CO_2)	Degradation of air quality	Yes	Impact of global environment	H
Recycled paper in printers	Conservation of landfill space	Yes	Impact on natural resources	H
Styrofoam cup use	Landfill space usage	Yes	Impact on local environment	M
Chemical spills and leaks	Soil and water contamination	Yes	Impact on local environment	H
Solvent storage	Soil and water contamination	Yes	Impact on local environment	M
Chemical air releases	Degradation of air quality	Yes	Impact of global environment	M-H
Oil fuel burning	Greenhouse gas creation	Yes	Impact on global environment (e.g., ozone depletion, climate change)	M-H

symbol-based prioritization process that relates to a level of significance where:

- H = Highest
- M-H = Medium-High
- M = Medium
- M-L = Medium-Low
- L = Lowest

How will your organization decide what is assigned an "H" prioritization? The decision may relate to levels of severity of the environmental aspect and its associated impact with respect to costs, business losses, risk to leave unattended, socially responsible image, customer demands, competitive forces, and many more decision factors. Every organization weighs each decision factor slightly differently; there is no right-or-wrong decision, thus, this evaluation is similar to many other decisions an organization will make. One key difference is that when dealing with environmental issues and impacts, the effect could be much farther reaching if a problem is left unattended or neglected or if the organization practices Greenwashing.

Step 5: Determine Which Aspects are Significant   Now it is time to fill in that final column in your table to identify which aspects are significant to the organization in its environmental sustainability efforts (see Table 4.5). This analysis is crucial to the creation of objectives and the Green initiatives to accomplish the organization's objectives and overall goal of environmental sustainability. Thus, determining what a significant environmental aspect/impact is will need input from many key players and participants within the organization. This decision will have to be handled with the aid of the steering committee, stakeholders and others within the organization.

What will be your organization's decision making process in determining what is significant to be assigned objectives and to have Green initiatives created to resolve negative environmental impacts and to enhance positive environmental impacts? To become an environmentally sustainable organization, one that is socially responsible and defies the practice of greenwashing, the organization will have to take bold actions and make eco-friendly decisions that will assist their organization in becoming more competitive in

Table 4.5 Establishing Aspect Significance to Organization

Environmental Aspect	Related to Environmental Sustainability Goal	Criteria of Significance	Level of Significance	Significant to Organization?
E-waste generation	Yes	Impact on local environment	H	Yes
E-waste recycling	Yes	Impact on local environment	H	Yes
Hydroelectric electricity usage	Yes	Impact on global environment (e.g., ozone depletion, climate change)	M	Yes
Vehicle air emissions (CO_2)	Yes	Impact of global environment	H	Yes
Recycled paper in printers	Yes	Impact on natural resources	H	Yes
Styrofoam cup use	Yes	Impact on local environment	M	No
Chemical spills and leaks	Yes	Impact on local environment	H	Yes
Solvent storage	Yes	Impact on local environment	M	Yes
Chemical air releases	Yes	Impact of global environment	M-H	Yes
Oil fuel burning	Yes	Impact on global environment (e.g., ozone depletion, climate change)	M-H	Yes

the new business landscape of Green market and consumers who will demand nothing less than buying from an organization that has achieved environmental sustainability status.

Create Short-Term and Long-Term Goals and Objectives

The next step of the planning process flow is to create short- and long-term goals and assign objectives to each. It is prudent to have both short- and long-term goals. An organization can offer quicker remediation to environmental impacts that need immediate resolution with short-term goals and to refer impacts that can withstand a longer remediation process to long-term goal assignments. This is also in alignment with the strategic goals of many organizations, which have both types of goal timelines. Furthermore, the ability to secure appropriate funding and resources and to meet different regulatory compliance timelines will also be a factor in the short- or long-term goal assignment.

Environmentally sustainable goals must have certain supporting characteristics:, stewardship, funding, and support from the organization from top to bottom of the organizational chart. Support is achieved through executive sponsorship, proper funding and prioritization, training and awareness, and alignment with the organization's overall strategic goal strategy. Some additional key aspects of goals that are to be defined:

- **Actionable.** Must be actionable—that is, there must be something that can be done to address the problem. For example, trying to ban the element uranium to stop nuclear power would be impossible, given the laws of nature. Green initiative efforts should be assignable and actionable, as to be able to complete the required tasks to achieve the overall goal. Defining goals that are not actionable may be seen by customers, governmental regulators, and Green watchdog groups as Greenwashing tactics.
- **Measureable.** Can be measured to establish progress. Measurable objectives are even more useful when they include specific targets.
- **Timely.** Must be achieved in the time planned and allotted. Do not pick a problem to resolve that is so far in the future that it is not relevant to anyone now.

- **Relevant.** The goal should be of interest and relevant to stakeholders and to the organization as a whole in its environmentally sustainable mission.
- **Important.** The goal must be something that is relevant to the organization and that it is willing to commit resources to achieve. Others will be less likely to join if you and your organization are not invested in the process as an initiator.

An outline of some key components can be used as a template for the goal definition. Components that could be part of a goal outline include:

- Statement
- Definition
- Scope and timeline
- Assumptions
- Constraints
- Achievability reference
- Organizational resources required
- Training and awareness needs
- Risk analysis

Now let's move on to some sample goals that can be extrapolated from the work that we have just done. These goals strive to meet the conditions discussed—they are actionable and relevant; they can be accomplished in a timely manner; and they are of importance to the organization with respect to environmental sustainability, social responsibility, and to show customers that it is taking actions and not establishing Greenwashing practices. Examples of goals, associated objectives, and actions are presented next.

Goal #1: Reduce Overall IT Data Center Power Usage and Increase Percentage of IT Data Center Alternative Energy Source Usage

Objective #1: Conserve Energy Used by Servers
- Actions:
  - Purchase ENERGY STAR 5.0 servers.
  - Reduce physical server count via server virtualization technology.

Objective #2: Obtain Higher Percentage of Electricity from Alternative Energy Sources
- Actions:
  - Install solar panel systems on IT data center facilities.
  - Plan for new IT data centers to be located near hydro-electric power plants or wind farms.

Goal #2: Increase E-Waste Recycling Efforts

Objective #1: Minimize E-Waste Negative Impacts of the Organization on the Environment
- Actions:
  - Set goal of e-waste recycling for organization to 75%.
  - Establish partnership with local e-waste recycling firm for all locations of e-waste generation.
  - Enhance organization's e-waste training and awareness program.

Objective #2: Think Globally and Act Locally by Promoting and Using IT Recycled or Refurbished Equipment
- Actions:
  - Set goal of purchasing IT recycled or refurbished equipment to 10% of overall IT equipment purchases, with the exception of printing cartridges being at least 75%.
  - Establish higher incentives within employee purchase plans of laptops and desktops for refurbished equipment.

IT Department Resource and Offering Requirements

After reviewing the sample goals and objectives from the last section, IT department resources and offerings that are both contributors to and participants in fulfilling the goals can take place, as shown in Table 4.6. These assignment resources are preliminary and will be solidified in the implementation stage with more granularity. The planning stage provides insight into the required offerings and resources that will assist in the budgeting, timeline, and risk analysis requirements of the environmental sustainability plan.

With the understanding and assessment of the IT resources and offerings within the organzation, we can categorize the IT offerings and resources. This will then allow for these offerings

Table 4.6   IT Department Resource and Offering Assignment: Contributor

Plan Need	IT Resource Category	IT Offering Category
Advising	Green IT advisors, IT architects, data center engineers	IT systems and data center design and management
Dashboards and scorecards	Directors and managers, Green IT advisors, data center engineers	IT systems and data center design and management
Web portals	Database administrators, custom application development	Tactical, operational, and strategic reporting
Data gathering, reporting, assessment	Database administrators, custom application development	Enterprise data management/master data management

and resources to be assigned to each goal and its corresponding objectives, shown in Table 4.7. A listing of possible IT resource and offering categories:

- Human resources
  - Green IT advisors
  - Directors and managers
  - IT architects
  - System architects
  - Data center engineers
  - Database administrators
  - Network engineers
  - System analysts
  - Application developers
  - Help desk/support
- Technology Resources
  - Data centers: power, cooling, hosting
  - Networks: intranet, Internet, extranet, mobile, wireless, wired.
  - Desktops/laptops
  - Servers: virtual/physical, file, print, application, database, management.

Table 4.7   IT Department Resource and Offering Assignment: Participator

Goal	Objective	IT Human Resource Category	IT Technology Resource Category	IT Offering Category
1	1	Green IT advisors, IT architects, data center engineers	Data center, servers	IT systems and data center design and management, Green IT assessment, procurement, and advising
1	2	Directors and managers, green IT advisors, data center engineers	Data center, servers	Green IT assessment, procurement and advising
2	1	Directors and managers, Green IT advisors, IT architects, system architects	Desktops/laptops, servers	Green IT assessment, procurement, and advising
2	2	Directors and managers, Green IT advisors, IT architects, system architects	Desktops/laptops, servers	Green IT assessment, procurement, and advising

- Disk storage: storage area network (SAN), network attached storage (NAS)
- Mobile devices: PDAs, cell phones.
- Backup/restore: tape units
- Offerings
  - Green IT assessment, procurement, and advising
  - Asset management
  - Application portfolio management
  - Custom application development
  - IT-business application design and planning
  - IT systems and data center design and management
  - Enterprise data management/master data management
  - Tactical, operational, and strategic reporting
  - Business intelligence analytics and predictive analysis

- Business performance management
- Auditing and regulatory compliance
- Project management

Plan Finalization and Revisions

During and after the planning stage, the organization may need to revise and modify the plan to dynamically adjust to organizational needs. Some concepts that may require plan modification:

- **ESTF feedback to steering committee.** Have a facility that allows for ESTF to offer feedback to the steering committee. This may be both a formal and an anonymous process.
- **Business benefits to organization.** New business opportunity, ability to increase market share, increase competitiveness, increase profitability.
- **Higher level of environmental benefits.** An increased productive benefit to the environment and to the overall goal of environmental sustainability for the organization.
- **Organizational merge and/or acquisition.** Organization is merged with or bought by another business, or buys another organization.
- **New regularity compliances enacted.** Local, national, or regional regulations are enacted that require compliance that was outside the scope of the original plan.
- **Funding priorities and economic factors.** Recession, decrease in profitability and revenue, stock price decline, interest rate increase, currency fluctuation.
- **New Green-related technologies.** IT, manufacturing, energy usage and consumption.

Changes in and to the planning stage will need to be completed in a systematic and disciplined manner. The result should offer the lowest impact with the greatest efficiency and effectiveness. Some key areas to address during the change review process include:

- **Change control process.** An official process of reviewing, implementing, approving, and managing changes to the plan.
- **Impact analysis.** What will the net effect of the change be (i.e., social, economic, political, environmental, business, costs, regulatory)?

- **Risk analysis.** What is the risk to the organization and environment to move forward or not, and on what timeline with the change?
- **Cost differential analysis.** What is the cost to the organization if the changes are to be implemented in comparison with the original projected plan budget?

The impact analysis may indicate that the organization will need proceed differently to implement the changes. Some possibilities of different implementation options are:

Planning Stage Still in Progress

- Modify the existing plan.
- Create a new plan and work both plans in parallel, with an eventual merger of the plans to occur.
- Create a new plan and work both plans in parallel, with no merger of the plans to occur.
- Close the existing plan and restart the planning stage.

Postplanning Stage

- Reopen the closed and signed-off plan, and append it as a revision to the plan.
- Keep the plan closed and create a new plan.

Planning Stage Tips

The planning stage has many moving parts and different levels of complexity within its processes, requires organizational commitment and integration, is in need of a productive and effective project management office, and can be complemented with the implementation of a project management application and architecture from the IT department. This chapter has defined a framework and processes that can be used as guidelines in your overall Green initiative efforts toward the goal of organizational environmental sustainability. Some additional planning stage tips are presented next.

- Prevent Greenwashing: plan to act and act responsibly.
- Align the plan with the overall environmental sustainability mission and policy.
- Think globally and act globally.
- Engage stakeholders and build partnerships.

- Bring internal and external players together early in the planning process.
- Gain and secure approval from upper management in the form of an official directive, policy, or mission statement.
- Ensure that the planning process is open, collaborative, and inclusive.
- Consider providing training, invoking research, and attending conferences and seminars to assist the planning stage in its analysis and decisions.
- Invite government officials, international associations, partners, and community groups to participate in the process. Strive to achieve and possibly exceed regulatory compliances.
- Make sure employees and staff are kept informed and seek their feedback. Establish formal, informal, and anonymous feedback paths and channels.
- Implement an EMS and utilize it through the entire planning stage.
- Select a project management software application and architecture that will support, enhance, and compliment the project planning management process.
- Implement reviews of project management features, needs, training required, costs, ease of use, integration with other systems, reporting, and much more to assist in the selection of the software application.
- Review the latest and greatest technology as well as what may be available 5, 10, and 25 years down the road.

Inevitably, a successful planning stage adheres to a disciplined, well-structured, and methodical planning process that incorporate best practices, lessons learned, outside consulting advice, internal and external review and auditing, and the will and support of the organization to create and carry the plan through.

Summary

Green initiative planning with the IT department is a series of defined and disciplined steps within a well-structured framework that utilizes the discipline of project management and the resources in the project management office and the IT department. Look to utilize an EMS and implement its capabilities and functionality during the planning stage.

Integrating the IT department's resources and offerings in the planning stage will be much more beneficial than waiting until later stages of the organization's Green initiative efforts. The IT department is one of the key contributors of an organization fulfilling its environmental sustainability goal. Participation in the planning stage will position IT resources and offerings within the Green initiative efforts in a way that maximizes them. Utilizing the IT department as a contributor, participant, and enabler can provide the organization's Green initiative efforts more functionality and capabilities.

The planning stage provides insight into the organization's environmental aspects and impacts. Insights gained during this stage enable the organization to categorize, prioritize, and select actionable objectives that will assist it in achieving environmental sustainability.

The success of the planning stage can be attributed to many factors—specifically, adherence to a disciplined, well-structured, and methodical planning process that incorporates best practices, lessons learned, outside consulting advice, internal and external review and auditing, and the will and support of the organization to create and carry the plan through. Additionally, the integration of PMO and IT department resources into the planning processes will increase the effectiveness and productiveness of the planning stage and later stages.

Notes

1. www.iso.org/iso/iso_14000_essentials
2. www.ci.minneapolis.mn.us/sustainability/environmentalteams.asp

5

Green Initiative
Implementation with IT

This chapter offers insight into the process of implementing a Green initiative with IT departmental resources and offerings in an effective manner. The integration of IT resources and offerings at certain points of the implementation stage, along with how the IT department can be engaged effectively during the process, is discussed, as is team unity and collaboration among IT and non-IT personnel.

Furthermore, the continued use of the environmental management system (EMS) and project management processes will be presented, and how they will effectively assist with the implementation of Green initiative projects. Productive and effective project management is the key to successful implementation of the Green initiative actions required to meet the organization's environmentally sustainable goals and objectives.

Implementation Stage Overview

What is required from the IT department to execute and complete the Green initiative actions to meet the organization's environmentally sustainability goals? The EMS shows the organization just how the IT department is necessary to execute the actions of each objective, manage and monitor the overall project, and much more. As in the planning stage, the IT department will have to provide offerings that are reliable, compliant, and cost effective and that continuously adapt to the ever-changing needs of the business, Green initiative projects, and new risks.

During the implementation stage, the business and the IT department continue to work as strategic partners to determine how the IT offerings will assist with enabling the organization to succeed. The IT department needs to be a positive influencing contributor, not a drain of the organization's effectiveness, productivity, and competiveness. Doing that requires a joint commitment from the chief executive officer and chief information officer that achieves:

- Understanding of the organization's environmental sustainability goals, their objectives, and required actions by the IT department and the entire organization that will need to be implemented and completed successfully to meet those goals
- Establishment of a business strategy and framework that defines how the current and future IT department offerings and resources strategically support strategic goals
- Defining and adhering to strong and disciplined reliability metrics and practices that relate to the effectiveness of the IT department's performance
- High-level executive and cross-department support, financing, cooperation, and collaboration among the IT department and business functions and needs

Green initiative implementation with the IT department provides continued value to the organization's environmental sustainability goals by taking action with selectively chosen IT offerings and resources to assist in the Green initiatives stage that will allow for stage completion with satisfactory results. It is in the implementation stage that the IT department is called to action as a participant in and contributor to the Green initiative effort.

Why is the IT department able to benefit during the implementation stage with action? The department is no stranger to enterprise- and organizational-wide projects. It is continuously engaged in many projects that utilize strong and disciplined project management concepts and practices. The interaction with the project management office, the allocation of resources, and the establishment of project funding and prioritization are all concepts that the IT department is well versed in. IT department resources are in most cases actionable by virtue of their role definition and the interaction they have with the business on a daily basis, thus are great fits to an implementation stage.

The implementation stage is more than just an environmental sustainability goal and integration of the IT department. Figure 5.1 offers insight into a formula that shows the IT department integration component of a Green initiative implementation effort along with the relationship of the EMS and project management as well as organizational strategic goals.

EMS and Project Management + IT Department Integration + Organizational Strategic Goals = Green Initiative Implementation with IT Department

The importance and necessity of the EMS—in many cases a system that has been put online with the aid of the IT department—

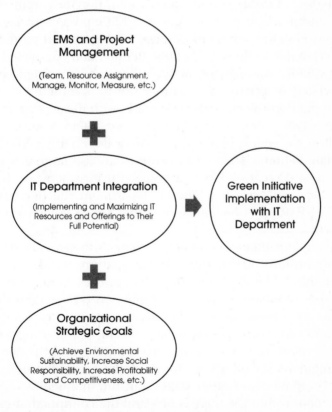

Figure 5.1   Formula for Green Initiative Implementation with IT

continues. The introduction of project management, along with continued use of the EMS, will be required in defining Green initiative projects and completing them effectively.

Implementation stage processes are a culmination of steps, procedures, and practices that need to be followed in a systematic and disciplined manner. They range from project management team formation and utilization, to IT resource and offering assignment.

Implementation Stage Process Flow

It is time to dive deeper into the implementation stage process flow. In this stage we will discuss the integration of the IT department as a contributor and participant. The IT department's contribution can be in the utilization of its technical and human resources along with the use of IT systems, databases, application development capabilities, and much more to support the EMS, project management, and the overall implementation stage. IT department participation will be related to actions that will be defined and completed within the EMS under each environmental sustainability related goal and its associated objective. IT resources will be assigned within each Green initiative project to particular tasks with the appropriate level of responsibility, guidance, capability, and integration. One such example is the action required regarding the energy consumption of IT data centers. These data centers can use large amounts of electricity and create a large carbon footprint when not designed in an eco-friendly manner. The IT department can purchase only ENERGY STAR 5.0 compliant servers that are designed to consume less power.

The implementation stage process flow, as shown in Figure 5.2, is a combination of systematic processes that are to take place serially but should be flexible, adaptable, and collaborative, as are other types of business processes implemented by organizations.

Some key components of the implementation process flow are the creation of a project management team; the drafting, creating and implementing of Green initiative projects; and the continued involvement of stakeholders. Some of these are continuing and similar components of other stages, but the uniqueness of project management within the stage is new and the continued integration of the IT department is enhanced.

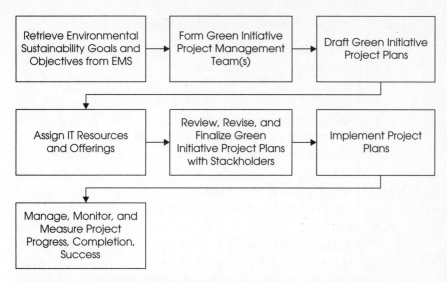

Figure 5.2   Implementation Stage Process Flow with IT Department

Retrieve Goals and Objectives from EMS

Going back to the EMS as the source of the organization's environmentally sustainable strategy, planning, and implementation facility will allow for review of the defined and stored goals and objectives. The actions you laid out in the planning stage are acted on in the implementation stage. Sample goals and objectives that were defined in Chapter 4 are presented next.

> **Goal #1: Reduce Overall IT Data Center Power Usage and Increase Percentage of IT Data Center Alternative Energy Source Usage**
>
> Objective #1: Conserve Energy Used by Servers
> - Actions:
>   - Purchase ENERGY STAR 5.0 servers.
>   - Reduce physical server count via server virtualization technology.
>
> Objective #2: Obtain Higher Percentage of Electricity from Alternative Energy Sources
> - Actions:
>   - Install solar panel systems on IT data center facilities.
>   - Plan for new IT data centers to be located near hydro-electric power plants or wind farms.

Goal #2: Increase E-Waste Recycling Efforts

Objective #1: Minimize E-Waste Negative Impacts of the Organization on the Environment
- Actions:
  - Set goal of e-waste recycling for organization to 75%.
  - Establish partnership with local e-waste recycling firm for all locations of e-waste generation.
  - Enhance organization's e-waste training and awareness program.

Objective #2: Think Globally and Act Locally by Promoting and Using IT Recycled or Refurbished Equipment
- Actions:
  - Set goal of purchasing IT recycled or refurbished equipment to 10% of overall IT equipment purchases, with the exception of printing cartridges being at least 75%.
  - Establish higher incentives within employee purchase plans of laptops and desktops for refurbished equipment.

Green Initiative Project Management Team

Project management concepts and components are used a great deal during the implementation stage. This is no different for projects related to Green initiatives. Many large organizations have established project management offices (PMOs) that are involved in the process of the creation of the Green initiative project management team. Other organizations may not have a PMO but rather have several project managers (PMs) who are available, may have a leader of the Green initiative project serve as PM, or utilize project management consulting firms or outsource the project management function.

There is great value in a PMO, for it is an entity that is structured, disciplined, and implements project management standards, certifications, and best practices. The PMO strives to standardize

---

Project Management Office

Department or group that defines and maintains the standards and processes related to project management within an organization.

Source: www.projectsmart.co.uk/project-management-office.html

and introduce economies of repetition in the execution of projects. The PMO is the source of documentation, guidance, and metrics on the practice of project management and execution. A good PMO will base project management principles on accepted and proven industry-standard methodologies, such as project management body of knowledge (PMBOK) or projects in controlled environments (PRINCE2). If your organization does not have a PMO, use a PM with these skill sets and capabilities to staff your Green initiative project management team:

- People friendly
- Managing cost and quality
- Managing risks and change
- Communicating with project stakeholders on the project's progress
- Attaining team objectives
- Planning work
- Allocating resources
- Defining tasks
- Assigning responsibility
- Controlling and monitoring quality
- Scrutinizing progress
- Checking performance
- Appointing secondary leaders
- Building and upholding team sprit
- Setting standards and maintaining regulation
- Training the team
- Setting up systems to facilitate communication with the team
- Developing work methods to craft team function cohesiveness
- Developing individuals
- Balancing team needs and task needs
- Balancing team needs and individual needs
- Performance appreciation and rewards
- Helping team members with personal problems
- Leadership skill to incite action, progress, and change
- Contractual skills to organize subcontractors
- Legal knowledge
- Evaluation of alternatives and ability for decision making
- Planning and controlling for necessary counteractive measures
- Financial familiarity for budget risk management

- High communication skills
- Negotiating abilities
- People management to motivate them toward the project goal
- System designing and maintenance

Beyond the PMO and the PM are additional key members of the Green initiative project team. They play an important role in the team's productivity and effectiveness by adding depth and breadth of business knowledge, cross-business function exposure, and business relationships. Assign members to the team who have had prior project management exposure, are team players, collaborate effectively, are respected among organizational departments and peers, and are driven to complete projects on time. These are key roles that comprise a Green initiative project:

- Project manager
- IT department environmental sustainability lead
- Business environmental sustainability lead
- Legal and regulatory representative
- Environmental sustainability steering committee representative
- Finance and budget representative
- Environmental sustainability partnership and alliances representative

Draft Green Initiative Project Plans

Green initiative projects will need to be framed to meet the goals defined, achieve the objectives associated with each goal, and complete each action by assigning resources, allotting time, and the like. This is to be done in a disciplined manner utilizing project management concepts, software, and best practices.

Project Management Structure and Procedures Define and document the structure, procedures, and processes of project management up front. Figure 5.3 offers insight into the main project management process areas. The document should include sections on how the team will manage issues, scope change, risk, resources, communication, delivery, tracking, auditing, reporting, and project management tools. It is important to manage the project rigorously and proactively and to ensure that the project

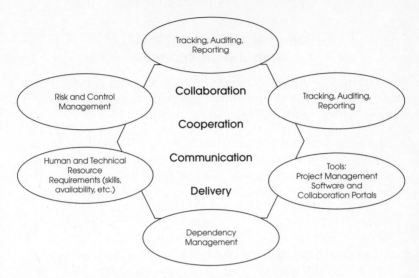

Figure 5.3   Project Management: Green Initiative Projects

team and all stakeholders have a common understanding of how the project will be managed. Effective collaboration, cooperation, communication, and delivery are core areas that will help your Green initiative projects be more successful.

If your organization needs to learn project management procedures, many associations, seminars, conferences, and consultants offer information. One such association is the Project Management Institute (PMI). Not only are those organizations who are embarking upon a more declined structure of project management, there are those organizations seeking to continuously perfect their project management processes and procedures, and this will be extremely beneficial to Green initiative projects.

Communication Plan   Communication is important for successful project management and communication planning attempts to answer these questions:

- How will information be stored?
- How will knowledge be stored?
- What information goes to whom, when, and how?
- Who can access what information?

Project Management Institute: Association Example

The Project Management Institute (PMI) is a leader in the establishment of project management best practices, training, and certification. According to the PMI Web site:

> PMI is the world's leading not-for-profit membership association for the project management profession, with more than half a million members and credential holders in 185 countries. Our worldwide advocacy for project management is supported by our globally-recognized standards and credentials, our extensive research program, and our professional development opportunities. These products and services are the basis of greater recognition and acceptance of project management's successful role in governments, organizations, academia and industries. PMI's core values are the fundamental and enduring principles that guide our actions and create a common language for our diverse group of global stakeholders.

Source: www.pmi.org/aboutus/pages/default.aspx

The communication plan is an essential supplement to the project work plan. When the work plan is being executed, the procedures and processes defined and agreed on in the communication plan are essential in ensuring that information and knowledge is being transferred among stakeholders, project team members, and many others. The communication plan is another area in which the involvement of the IT department will be very beneficial. The IT department can offer project portals, collaborative Web sites, and messaging systems and equipment that will be used as part of the communication plan. IT offerings are only some of the communication plan's resources. Face-to-face meetings may occur as well.

Project Definition and Work Plan   Once the project management procedures are established and agreed on, the Green initiative projects will need to have a project definition document drafted that takes the outcomes of the planning stage and allows for the creation of the project work plan.

Verify that the project definition document for your Green initiative projects have the next structure and information, which will be essential in creating the work plan:

- **Project Overview**. Why is the project taking place? What are the business drivers? What are the business benefits?
- **Objectives**. What will be accomplished by the project? What do you hope to achieve?
- **Scope**. What deliverables will be created? What major features and functions will be implemented? What organizations will be converted? What is specifically out of scope?
- **Assumptions and Risks**. What events are you taking for granted (assumptions), and what events are you concerned about? What will you do to manage the risks to the project?
- **Approach**. Describe how the project will unfold and proceed.
- **Organization**. Show the significant roles on the project. The project manager is easy, but who is the sponsor? Who is on the project team? Are any of the stakeholders represented?
- **Signature Page**. Ask the sponsor and key stakeholders to approve this document, signifying that they are in agreement with what is planned.
- **Initial Effort, Cost, and Duration Estimates**. These should start as best-guess estimates and then be revised, if necessary, when the work plan is completed.

After the project definition has been prepared, the work plan can be created. The work plan provides the step-by-step instructions for constructing project deliverables and managing the project. Use a prior work plan from a similar project as a model, if one exists. If not, build one the old-fashioned way by utilizing a work-breakdown structure and network diagram.

Create both a high-level and a detailed work plan, assigning resources and estimating the work. The high-level work plan is for those who need only a summary view of what is to be accomplished, by whom, costs, and how long it will take. The much more detailed work plan is used by those who are closer to or actually are performing the required tasks. A lower level of granularity will give you much greater detail and more breakdowns to task and subtask levels. You could extrapolate a summary high-level work plan from the detailed plan by using the feature in project management software that rolls up the details and shows the summary information.

The work plan should remove vagueness, ambiguity, and any other doubts. It is similar to a blueprint for construction of a building, one that contains enough information so that someone walking off the street could begin building with few or no questions.

Project Management Software   Project management software can aid in Green initiative project creation, definition, work planning,

Microsoft Project 2010: Software Example

Microsoft Project Server 2010, built on SharePoint Server 2010, delivers flexible work management solutions. These innovative capabilities in Project Server 2010 lead to improved productivity and better business performance:

- **Unified project and portfolio management**. Familiar SharePoint user interface and a common data store make Project Server 2010 easy to use. A comprehensive Application Programming Interface (API) enables you to customize and extend both project and portfolio capabilities.
- **Effective use of resources**. Select the right project portfolios and maximize resource utilization—effectively prioritizing projects from multiple dimensions.
- **Flexible Web-based project editing**. Easily build schedules online and conveniently make project edits from anywhere.
- **Demand management simplified**. Capture all work from simple tasks to complex projects in a centralized repository. Develop and deploy effective governance workflows to drive accountability and capture project information, cost and resource estimates, and other valuable project data.
- **More powerful dashboards and reports**. Gain transparency and control with the Microsoft Business Intelligence Platform: Excel Services, PerformancePoint Services, Visio Services, PowerPivot for Excel 2010, and SQL Reporting Services are all at your fingertips. Customize reports in a familiar Excel editor and create powerful dashboards to effectively monitor and share portfolio performance.

Source: http://technet.microsoft.com/en-us/library/ff686783.aspx

and management by offering a rich set of features and capabilities. Capabilities include scheduling, cost control and budget management, resource allocation, collaboration, communication, reporting, and many more that are related to the needs of Green initiative projects. Microsoft Project is one such project management program.

Costs, time, and resources are three variables for project management. Organization resources are scarce, typically overbooked and overworked, and in many cases they are globally dispersed. Budgets are being reduced and scrutinized more than ever before due to stiff competition, downturns in the global economy, and global financial instability. Organizations are reducing the time allotted for project completion as time to market is a factor in increasing competitiveness and profitability. Thus, effective and productive project management is more crucial than ever. Figure 5.4 shows a view into a project's costs using project management software.

The expense of purchasing, implementing, and training users on the project management software should yield substantial benefits to your organization and projects. Project management software has the ability not only to manage your costs but also to improve your cost and time estimates.

Figure 5.4   Project Management Software: Managing Costs

Create a list of requirements that your Green initiative projects will need from project management software to use when talking with vendors. A sample is shown next.

- Task lists for people and allocation schedules for resources
- Overview information on how long tasks will take to complete
- Early warning of any risks to the project
- Information on workload for planning holidays and training
- Historical information on how projects have progressed; in particular, how actual and planned performance are related
- Optimum utilization of available resource
- Scheduling, shown in Figure 5.5
- Calculating critical path
- Desktop and Web-based interfaces
- Personal and collaborative environments
- Integrated offering with EMS, project planning, change control management, customer relationship management, messaging and communication systems

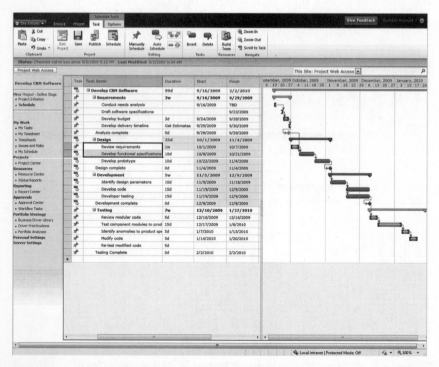

Figure 5.5   Project Management: Scheduling

Project planning software provides information to various stakeholders and can be used to measure and justify the level of effort required to complete the project. Furthermore, it will assist an organization in gaining visibility and control across all work, enhancing decision making, improving alignment with business strategy, maximizing resource utilization, and enhancing project execution to optimize return on investment.

Assign IT Resources and Offerings

Green initiative projects with IT department integration will utilize human and technical resources as well as offerings. The project scope, requirements, budget, duration, and capabilities will determine the extent and types of IT department resources and offerings needed. The selection and assignment of IT department resources is as crucial as their utilization, maximization, and availability.

Looking at human resources, employees are the most valuable asset and the biggest expense for most organizations. The ability to deploy employees effectively against often conflicting Green initiative projects and other work priorities enables organizations to optimize their return on human resource investments. To maximize productive levels of project task efforts and employee morale, resource and PMs need an efficient project management system to place the appropriate staff on the right teams at the right time.

IT department resource demands will have to be assessed across the organization so Green initiative PMs can make staffing decisions to support environmental sustainability goals and objectives. You must understand which Green initiative projects and types of work are consuming the most valuable IT resources in order to align resource allocation plans based on changing priorities and budgets. Get the most from your most valuable resources and quickly correct critical path tasks that are overdue by assigning resources based on skill requirements and level of proficiency.

Let's look at the list of human and technical resources that are available for Green initiative projects:

- Human resources
  - Green IT advisors
  - Directors and managers
  - IT architects
  - System architects

- Data center engineers
- Database administrators
- Network engineers
- System analysts
- Application developers
- Help desk/support
- Technology resources
  - Data centers: power, cooling, hosting
  - Networks: intranet, Internet, extranet, mobile, wireless, wired
  - Desktops/laptops
  - Servers: virtual/physical, file, print, application, database, management
  - Disk storage: storage area network (SAN), network attached storage (NAS)
  - Mobile devices: PDA, cell phones
  - Backup/restore: tape units
- Offerings
  - Green IT assessment, procurement, and advising
  - Asset management
  - Application portfolio management
  - Custom application development
  - IT-business application design and planning
  - IT systems and data center design and management
  - Enterprise data management/master data management
  - Tactical, operational, and strategic reporting
  - Business intelligence analytics and predictive analysis
  - Business performance management
  - Auditing and regulatory compliance

IT-related resources can be assigned from the organization's internal IT department and outsourcing. In outsourcing, IT tasks are performed with an external vendor for the benefit of the contracting organization.

Outsourcing

Procurement of services from an external vendor that may be offering and/or hosting services locally, regionally, or globally distant.

Outsourcing has different options and implementations that offer operating models for organizations to engage external vendors:

- **Homeshoring**. The use of vendors in the same country. The benefits may be the ability to better coordinate across time-zone differences with fewer language and cultural barriers and to make in-person meetings to check on progress more easily.
- **Offshoring**. The use of distant foreign countries that host IT services. The benefit may be lower costs for IT services. The challenges may be time zones, language and cultural barriers, and the ability to physically review progress and meetings.
- **Nearshoring**. The use of much closer foreign countries that host and perform IT services. An example would be a shift of U.S. organizations from using India and China to using Canada and Latin America. Benefits may be lower IT costs, fewer time-zone differences, and fewer language and cultural barriers.

After the resources for the Green initiative project have been selected, approved, and procured, it is time to build the project team by entering the resource information into the project plan. Doing this will set the stage for later assigning team members to specific tasks within the project schedule. For now, let's get the resources entered and start creating a resource pool that will allow for the administration of people or equipment to be assigned to. The resource pool centralizes resource information, such as the resource name, calendar used, resource units, and cost rate tables.

Functions of Microsoft Project 2010 that relate to entering resource information into the project are presented next.[1]

- **Add resources to your project team**. Add enterprise resources and details, such as group, resource type, skills, and maximum units. Add resources to your project to add enterprise and nonenterprise resources to the team. Substitute resources to replace an enterprise resource in the project with another enterprise resource (outside current team) or with a generic resource.
- **Set working times for the project and resources**. Set up the availability for all resources in the project as well as individual resources by setting working times. Indicate vacations, standard and nonstandard work schedules, and different resource

units. Specify resource availability to control how much time a work resource is available.

- **Change information for enterprise resources**. Make changes to the resource information (i.e., apply a new calendar, costs, or skills to the resource).
- **Add resource skills**. Add a custom field for resource skills to the resource sheet. Filter, sort, or group on this field to identify resources by their skills by skill codes.
- **Set resource costs**. Enter rates and fees for people, equipment, and materials to create a budget or to track project costs.
- **Set up lines of communication**. Team members and stakeholders can collaborate online via e-mail, conference calls, team collaboration sites, etc.
- **Add supporting information about resources**. Add more information about resources in the form of notes or documents or by viewing the resource reports.

Now it is time to start taking each task and action within the Green initiative project and assigning IT department resources and offerings per line item. This level of granularity is required for detailed IT department resource and offering allocation requests and assignments. Without this level of granularity, the Green initiative project will not be able to complete the required tasks; thus it will not be able to fulfill its objectives and meet its goals. This is where to check to see whether any resources are overallocated or underallocated, to add notes, and to communicate assignments to team members. These functions can be performed by Microsoft Project 2010 during resource assignments:

- Assign a resource. Assignments are the associations between specific tasks and the resources needed to complete them. More than one resource can be assigned to a task. Both work resources and material resources can be assigned to tasks.
- Refine resource assignments by making adjustments to the assignments that you made, check for overallocations, and perhaps resolve overallocations by leveling.
  - Assign an additional resource to a task to refine an assignment, especially if another resource is overallocated or needs assistance to complete a task on time.
  - Replace a resource assignment to help balance the workload for specific assignments. Doing so can help control costs

when replacing an expensive resource with a less expensive one. And you can increase quality, where needed, if replacing a lower-quality resource with a higher-quality one.

- Remove a resource assignment if a resource is overallocated during a certain period of time.
- Reassign the remaining work on a task to control which of several resources do what portion of the remaining work, or to specify exactly when the remaining work will be done.
- Resolve resource overallocations by leveling to even out the resource workload. The leveling process reschedules by using available slack time, splitting tasks, and adding delay until the overallocations are resolved. Note that leveling often can push out the project's finish date.
- Add a note about resource assignments by attaching a note, perhaps to describe project constraints or assumptions. Add a note to a task, resource, or project.
- Update resource information in a resource pool. If using resources from a resource pool, you can update their assignment information so that all the information is visible in the resource pool. This can help the project manager or resource manager check for overallocations across multiple projects. Share resources by using a resource pool.
- Communicate new assignments to affected resources either by making available assignment reports.

Stakeholder Management

Communicating with and managing the project's stakeholders is essential in the success of the project. It is an aspect of Green initiative project management that is to not be taken lightly, for your stakeholders hold the funding and approval for the project. In essence, they can make or break the project. This is not meant to make you afraid of your stakeholders but rather so that you understand what their needs are and that you must be able to communicate effectively with them. Common interactions with Green initiative project stakeholders include:

- Obtaining feedback on project status, funding, deliverables
- Offering workshops on project dashboard usage, key performance indicators (KPIs), scorecard, and reports

- Discussing and managing changes to project scope, funding, and timelines
- Offering demonstrations on project deliverables where applicable

During both the project planning stage and the implementation stage, you must determine who your project stakeholders are. A list of possible stakeholders for Green initiative projects includes:

- Project sponsors
- Environmental sustainability steering committee members
- Business unit and line managers
- Project team members
- Outside consultants, contractors, vendors
- Departments supplying resources and offerings (such as the IT department)

With new personnel joining Green initiative projects at various times and stages, there is a need to tell everyone involved who the stakeholders are. You can do this by pointing personnel to the project team collaboration site on your organization's intranet, by calling a formal meeting, or in other ways. Whatever the process, you must understand that the stakeholders have an interest in the project outcome. Unfortunately, in some cases, stakeholders may have conflicting interests. One or more stakeholders may want to see the project succeed; others may want it to fail. The ones who want it to succeed will see benefit to them; those who may want the project to fail will see it as a nuisance, burden, and hindrance to them. Watch for and identify hidden agendas.

Thus, there is a subset managing within project management called stakeholder management. Your stakeholders will need to be managed through every stage of your project. Start with involving them in clarifying the scope of your project and identifying possible solutions to the organization's problem that the project is designed to solve. As the project proceeds, draw up a communication strategy and plan that identifies how, when, and what to communicate to each stakeholder group. Part of doing this involves project reporting. How and when and to what level of detail will you deliver project reports to each group?

Stakeholders are an integral part of a project. They can be the end users or clients, the people from whom requirements will be drawn, the people who will influence the design, and, ultimately, the people who will reap the benefits of your completed project. Thus, it is extremely important to involve stakeholders in all stages of your project for two reasons.

1. Experience shows that their involvement in the project significantly increases your chances of success by building in a self-correcting feedback loop.
2. Involving them in your project builds confidence in your product and will greatly ease its acceptance by your target audience.

Different stakeholders will want very different outcomes from your project. A vital part of stakeholder management is managing these competing expectations from the initial stage through to final implementation. Finally, in the evaluation stage of your project, find out from your stakeholders how well the project satisfied their needs. You will learn valuable lessons for future projects.

Building relationships is just as important within the project team as it is outside. Good relationships can be the difference between outstanding success and dismal failure; it's all about getting people to like and trust you so that they will deliver what you need them to deliver at the right time in the right way. We have talked previously about managing stakeholders, finding out about and managing their needs and expectations. Doing this is much easier if you have developed good relationships with stakeholders in the first place.

Finalize Green Initiative Project Plans

The process of finalizing the Green initiative project plans with stakeholders and others in the approval process could present organization politics, hidden agendas, negative influences that can torpedo the project, and much more to the process. Keep in mind that one or more stakeholders may have a negative view on your organization's Green initiative projects. Take this into consideration every time you interact with them and ask for feedback and approval.

Furthermore, with projects related to environmental sustainability, external entities also could pose challenge the approval of the project (i.e., government regulations, shift in consumer demands, instability in local and global economies, geopolitical events, etc.). It will take a skilled PM to deal with all of these issues and challenges and to find ways to head them off and turn negatives into positives. Nevertheless, you can accomplish the process of finalizing and having the projects signed off, budgeted, and able to move to the next stage.

Implement Green Initiative Project Plans

The execution of the Green initiative projects typically is the longest component of the implementation stage and of the entire project management life cycle. Furthermore, execution consumes the majority of resources allocated to the project, including time, people, equipment, and money.

Work includes the physical construction of each deliverable that is going to be presented to the customer. These deliverables form the body of work that was agreed to with the customer at the outset of the project. During work execution, emphasis should be placed on communication in order to make decisions as quickly as possible if problems arise. Thus, the project can be accelerated by setting up a communication plan.

Project execution is characterized by the actual work on the tasks planned. Project control involves the comparison of the actual performance with the planned performance and taking appropriate corrective action to get the desired output. During execution, the project team is responsible for the activities listed next:

- Team members execute the tasks as planned by the PM.
- The PM is responsible for performance measurement, which includes finding variances between planned and actual work, costs, and schedules.
- The PM is responsible for providing the project status report to all key stakeholders to give them visibility into the project.
- Project key stakeholders are responsible for reviewing the metrics and variances.
- Project key stakeholders are responsible for taking necessary action on the variances to assist with completion of the project within time and budget.

Communication Plan Invocation   The communication plan that was agreed on earlier in the implementation stage is now invoked. It is here where actual meetings, storage, and movement of information and knowledge occur with project team members and stakeholders. The PM should set up regular meetings (i.e., weekly is preferred) in order to manage the project team by regularly discussing project progress and determining the priorities for the following weeks.

Time should be blocked in project team members' calendars for collaboration, discussions, and meetings. A work and communications balance will have to be developed to effectively and productively utilize each area. Too many meetings and communications can hinder work efforts; similarly, working in a vacuum and not communicating could be detrimental and counterproductive to the project.

Deliverables   During execution of the work plan, the building and creation of the project's deliverables will begin. Deliverables can take many forms (e.g., reports, new construction, regulatory compliance, a working model or prototype that demonstrates the principle involved). The deliverables will be measured, monitored, and go through a validation and approval process.

Because a deliverable is a tangible and measurable result, outcome, or product that is to be produced to complete a project or part of a project, the deliverable becomes a crucial aspect of a project's success. The deliverables will assist in ensuring that the project outcomes meet all stakeholder expectations and that the Green initiative project's goals align with the organization's larger environmental sustainability goal.

One key reminder is that a prototype is not to be considered a final product. If you present a prototype when a final product is the required, measurable, and approvable deliverable, issues will arise with your stakeholders.

This is where what was promised in the development of the Green initiative project definition and high-level work plan actually is delivered. There may be times where what was promised cannot be delivered at all, even with some modifications, additional funding, additional resources, more time, and so on.

Deliverables should be under a quality management plan that ensures that certain standards, requirements, and functionality are at least fulfilled and possibly superseded. Types of standards and requirements that may be associated with an organization's Green initiative deliverables are listed next.

- International Organizational for Standardization (ISO)
- Six Sigma
- United Nation Environmental Treaties
- Local, state, and national regulations and laws (i.e., U.S. Environmental Protection Agency)
- Greenhouse gas emissions: cap and trade

Deliverable quality can fall into many different categories to ensure deliverable usefulness and their ability to fulfill business requirements, assist with strategic objectives, and so on. A list of these types of quality-related categories is presented next.

- Reliability
- Usability
- Performance
- Customer response
- Conformance
- Maintainability
- Manageability

Status Report   Creating status reports can be viewed as time consuming and detrimental to the work that needs to be performed. But a status report to the PM, team leads, stakeholders, and others can be of substantial value in their analysis of the project's progress. A status report provides the organization with this information for a given reported time period:

- What has each project member been doing?
- Where are the tasks being performed?
- Have any critical paths been encountered?
- What dependencies have been identified?
- How have project resources (people, time, money, materials) been utilized?
- What do you still need to do to complete the project? What specific tasks are remaining?

- Will assigned tasks be completed for the project according to the original schedule?
- What adjustments may be needed to the project plan?
- What problems have been encountered, and how are they being addressed?

The status report will need to refer back to the assigned task definition, requirements, and schedule to compare progress, expectations, results, and the project schedule deadlines. Each status report will have some level of granularity with these types of details. Individual status reports will be much more detailed. A rolled-up and aggregated status report to a stakeholder is less granular in task-level details.

Once a Green initiative project has begun, the responsibility for updating team leads, the PM, and stakeholders will be assigned to various individuals. Having status reports completed on time is crucial. Every time a project team member status report is delayed, there will be a delay in the aggregated status report or the information will not be included. Thus project decision makers will have an incomplete picture of the status.

The progress report is also a place where issues can be raised and flagged. Waiting until the completion of a critical issue may not be as productive as alerting your respective lead before status report completion. A more timely process may be required to notify others of the issue. Some individuals may feel that the use of status reports to flag and raise issues is less effective and appropriate due to the current work environment, office politics, fear of physical communication, and so on.

Nevertheless, create and implement a productive and effective means of creating status reports (i.e., using a similar template), delivering status reports, (i.e., via a Web portal), and reporting when status reports have been delivered. Offer training sessions, demonstrations, and one-on-one meetings to assist in the process.

Manage, Monitor, and Measure Projects

The need to manage, monitor, and measure project efforts, statuses, budgets, and resource utilization can be achieved with the aid of a dashboard consisting of scorecard(s), performance indicators, thresholds, reports with charts, and gauges. These dashboards can be used by the PM, PMO, project team members, and stakeholders. Typically, different dashboard content is displayed to the different groups.

Project monitoring should also include alerts and notifications when certain thresholds fall below an acceptable and/or critical level; thus the project is proactive rather than discussing problems in status meetings after the fact. Green initiative project status meetings can head off project issues, but using alerts and notifications is advised.

The next areas related to management, monitoring, and measurement encompasses the work plan, risks, budget, and scope.

Manage the Work Plan Review the work plan with participants, leads, and stakeholders on a regular basis to determine how you are progressing in terms of schedule, resources, dependency, critical paths, and budget. The frequency of these review sessions may vary due to project status and different types of participants. Implement change control processes that will assist implemented required changes to the work plan based on identification of benefits, gains, or regulatory requirements.

Monitor the Schedule   Watch the project schedule like a hawk at every level of detail and progress. Establish time periods to review the schedule, update statuses, and determine risks to the schedule. Identify activities that have been completed during the previous time period and update the work plan to show that they are finished. After the work plan has been updated, determine if the updates reflect whether the project will be completed within the original effort, assigned resources, dependencies, cost, and duration. If not, determine the critical path and look for ways to adjust, accelerate, and adapt project tasks and activities to get the project schedule back on track.

Monitor the Budget Constant monitoring of the amount of money actually being used by the entire project, specific tasks, and groups of tasks is of utmost importance not only to the PM but also to many on the project team. Keeping costs down and staying on budget or under budget should be the key focus area. One way to monitor the budget is to determine whether the actual spending is more than estimated based on the work that has been completed. This process should be proactive, and risks impacting on staying on budget should be flagged. Budget KPIs are typically displayed in project scorecards and dashboards.

Monitor for Warning Signs Implement proactive monitoring for warning signs across all aspects of project management, the project schedule, deliverables, and risks from the very beginning of the Green initiative project's efforts. A plan to deal with alerting and notifying people of these warnings should also be implemented. Some examples of possible warnings to watch for are listed next.

- Schedule variances that seem to be minor but can cascade to become larger impacts on the project schedule.
- Remaining budget is below operating and projected thresholds.
- Spike in budget expenditures during a projected modest and smooth release of funds.
- Discovery that activities that reported as complete are still being worked on with assigned resources.
- Delay in equipment and materials from vendors and suppliers.
- Delay of configuration and setup of equipment and facilities within the organization.
- Need to rely on unscheduled overtime to meet deadlines.
- Reallocation of project resources to unexpected personnel issues.
- Stakeholder, PM, and other team member support and morale starts to decline.
- Deliverable quality or service quality starts to become unacceptable to deliverable acceptance criteria.

Manage Scope Scope creep, unmanageable and uncontrollable scope, and team members' inability to clearly understand the project scope can lead to project failure. Managing project scope is just as important and critical as managing the project schedule. Ensure that project scope creep and spin-offs on deliverables are not occurring. An example of spin-off deliverables are those that were not part of the approved and signed-off version of the project scope; they were created to satisfy some particular need and possibly consumed unscheduled resources and unallocated budget.

Project scope is approved by the project sponsors and is to be maintained by the PM. During a project, sometimes project sponsors request changes to the project scope, due to newly recognized and urgent business requirements. Understanding that the funding of the project is in the stakeholders' jurisdiction, and that they may seem to believe that change is acceptable and part of doing business is part of being a PM. The project scope should have defined and approved processes and procedures in place to accept changes to project scope and determine the impact of such changes (i.e., budget, project schedule, additional resources, etc.).

A disciplined and well-structured PMO, PM, and project management process will understand how to invoke scope change management procedures. These processes will determine the level of scope creep that can be allowed at certain times of the project, the procedures for requesting scope changes and getting them approved, and the ability to quickly integrate them into the project schedule.

Modifying the scope to be accommodating or to win over management with short-term flexibility can cause longer-term challenges and possibly project failure. Stick to a disciplined process of accepting, reviewing, and approving changes to the project scope. Perform a risk assessment of project scope changes and determine their impact to the existing project.

Manage Risk Implement and utilize a risk management process from the very beginning of a Green initiative project to its completion. Risks are potential events or circumstances outside the project team's control that will have an adverse impact on the project. Limit the effect of risks by avoiding mistakes of not understanding the benefits of risk management, not providing adequate time for risk management, and not identifying and assessing risk using a standardized and discipline approach.

From the beginning of Green initiative project definition, risk management should identify the risks to the organization, customers, regulatory compliance, and much more. This process continues through project planning, budgeting, assignment of resources and offerings from the IT department, and into the execution of work during the implementation stage. The project team should have a mechanism for reporting risks.

Risks can be assessed as they relate to impact on the project, the organization, the overall goal of environmental sustainability, and other categorization techniques. Specific plans should be put into place to mitigate those events identified as high risk to ensure that they do not, in fact, occur. Medium risks should be evaluated to see if they should be proactively managed as well. (Low-level risks may be identified as assumptions. That is, there is potential risk involved, but you are "assuming" that the positive outcome is much more probable.)

Once the risks have been identified and assessed, creating a strategy for acting on and dealing with them is the next step. General risk strategies include:

- **Reactive:** Accept the risk and act on it.
- **Avoidance:** Avoid and ignore the risk completely.
- **Proactive:** Reduce the likelihood or impact of the risk if it occurs.
- **Transferability:** Transfer the risk to another entity.

The process of monitoring risks occurs throughout the entire life cycle of Green initiative projects. Thus, continue to assess potential risks from beginning to end. The types of risk management that your organization puts in place should be tailored to particular parts of the project life cycle.

Manage Conflicts Even with effective risk management, reducing and eliminating project scope creep, and having project dashboards that display current statuses, issues that need to be handled and resolved still will arise. These issues can become conflicts when change is imposed, resistance is established, and disagreements fester. The collecting, storing, prioritizing, and reporting of project issues are functions of a project management application tool (i.e., Microsoft Project 2010). The need to incorporate conflict management processes should also be reviewed to determine priorities, impact, and other criteria that should be assessed to handle a conflict.

Blake and Mouton describe five approaches for dealing with conflict:

1. Withdrawing (low concern for both people and productivity)
2. Smoothing (high concern for people and low concern for productivity

3. Forcing (low concern for people and high concern for productivity)
4. Problem solving (high concern for both people and productivity)
5. Compromising (moderate concern for both people and productivity)[2]

Measure Progress   Part of the project processes and procedures the organization has agreed to implement and adhere to requires the measuring of the Green initiative project's progress, status, and metrics. Implement a Green Initiative project dashboard and scorecard for stakeholders and others to review project KPIs. Different dashboards showing different metrics or varying levels of granularity may serve the need of high-level management, stakeholders, and project management staff. Types of project performance metrics to measure include:

- **Total capacity**. Tells you how many potential hours staff is available to work.
- **Utilization rate**. Percentage of time that people are actually allocated to operations, support, projects, and discretionary.
- **Work allocation**. Actual versus targets: shows allocating work versus your target balancing.
- **Project: estimated budget versus actual**. Basic financial numbers that should be tracked for each project in the portfolio and then rolled up at the portfolio level.
- **Project: estimated deadline versus actual**. Estimated or planned time is projected and considered the baseline, which is compared with actual deadlines that are tracked and reflect how the tasks actually were accomplished.
- **Rework**. Reported from the project teams.
- **Client satisfaction**. Projects and operations and support teams should report some kind of customer satisfaction metrics.
- **Project benefits realization**. Reported by project sponsors and operations managers. All projects and programs have some business benefit. After each project is completed, the benefits should be tracked to ensure they are realized as proposed in the initial business case.

Implementation Stage Tips

A list of tips, comments, and strong recommendations is presented next.

- Compare your organization's project management procedures and processes with those of the Project Management Institute.
- Utilize stakeholder management processes and procedures.
- Utilize change management processes and procedures to record formal changes to project scope.
- Utilize risk management to record and monitor all risks within the project. Create a risk resolution strategy that offers both a proactive and reactive approach to handle current and possible conflicts in the future.
- Create and implement a communications plan and quality management plan.
- Utilize issue management by recording all issues within the project and prioritizing and resolving them in a timely manner.
- Select and utilize a project management tool (i.e., Microsoft Project 2010).
- Manage, measure, and monitor project KPIs statuses, deliverables, and much more.
- Handle conflicts with effective conflict management processes that consider personnel, products, organizational goals, and Green initiative project deadlines and commitments.

Summary

This chapter offered insight into the Green initiative implementation stage with aid of the IT department resources and offerings during project definition, resource assignments, and task execution. The integration of IT resources and offerings at particular areas of the implementation process, along with how the IT department can be effectively engaged as both a contributor and participant, were discussed. Furthermore, team unity and collaboration among IT and non-IT personnel throughout implementation were mentioned as well.

The introduction of a project management software tool was mentioned in conjunction with continued use of the EMS. The project management tool complements a well-defined and disciplined project management process and procedures, which can be found within an organization PMO, project management associations, and so on.

Throughout the implementation stage, the project is managed, monitored, and measured with respect to risks, conflicts, budget, resources, warnings, and much more. Doing this is crucial to ensure the completion of a productive and effective project management cycle that creates Green initiative deliverables that meet quality criteria.

Notes

1. Microsoft. (2010). Goal: Build the project team. http://office.microsoft.com/en-gb/project/HA102211571033.aspx
2. R. Blake and J. Mouton, *The Managerial Grid: The Key to Leadership Excellence* (Houston: Gulf Publishing Co., 1964).

CHAPTER 6

Green Initiative Assessment with IT

This chapter offers insight into how to assess the organization's Green initiatives with respect to achieving environmental sustainability and other strategic goals related to enhancing social responsibility, improving customer satisfaction, and increasing competiveness with the aid of the IT department's resources and offerings. The use of Balanced Scorecards displaying key performance indicators (KPIs), dashboards offering effective and productive data visualization that display metrics related to the goal objective's assessment criteria, and external reports for regulatory compliance are a few of the offerings from the IT department.

Assessment is also in the form of audits, stakeholder and customer feedback surveys, and other tools that will provide insight into the return on investment (ROI) of the organization's Green initiative efforts from a strategic viewpoint. IT-related offerings, such as reports and dashboards can assist with creating graphical visualization of pertinent assessment results onto the desktop computer screens of executives and others within the organization.

In this stage, the use of performance management processes and tools can be implemented as to monitor the KPIs related to environmental sustainability and Green initiative project results and expectations. Knowing how well each Green initiative effort has benefited the organization will aid in determining the future direction and continuance of Green initiative efforts.

Assessment Stage Overview

Organizations need to assess the outcome of their Green initiative efforts to evaluate their benefits. The assessment of each project budget, completion status, and funding is not sufficient. Rather, what is required is a strategic assessment of how Green initiative effort has benefited the organization with respect to increasing competitiveness, level of social responsibility, profitability, and regulatory compliance. For example, having one Green initiative effort in one geographical location of business operations fulfill one particular government regulation does not mean there is government compliance throughout an organization's global business operations.

To be successful, effective, and productive, the IT department must help in the execution of a Green initiative assessment that encompasses the entire organization. Also required are the continued use of the environmental management system (EMS) and some additional IT department offerings that will allow for visualization and reporting of environmental performance indicators (EPIs).

Environmental Performance Indicators (EPIs)

Include both managerial measures about management's efforts to influence environmental performance, such as number of projects and allocated budgets, as well as operational measures for results, such as usage rates of energy and water.

Source www.information-management.com

As was the case in the other stages, the IT department's offerings must be reliable, easy to use and access, compliant, and cost effective and must continuously adapt to the ever-changing needs of the business, Green initiative efforts, and government regulations. In the assessment stage, business and the IT department continue to work as strategic partners to determine how IT department resources and offerings will assist the organization to assess all of its Green initiative efforts and how close the organization is to achieving environmental sustainability. The IT department needs to be a positive and constructive contributor, not a drain of the organization's effectiveness, productivity, and competiveness throughout the assessment stage. Some tips for the IT department that will enhance IT-business relationship during this stage are presented next.

- Understand the organization's environmental sustainability goals with respect to objective criteria and established metrics.
- Be proactive in offering insight on how IT department offerings and resources can strategically support this stage with respect to data visualization and external reporting.
- Create IT department–related metrics that assess the benefits of the department's contribution to this stage and compare it with how the business evaluates its contribution.
- Continue to offer high-level executive and cross-department support, cooperation, and collaboration among IT and non–IT department and business functions and needs.

Green initiative assessment with the integration of the IT department can provide value to the organization if done with cohesiveness, accountability, and transparency. The IT department and the business must partner to achieve environmental sustainability for the entire organization. The assessment stage requires ethical, professional, and auditable processes that will allow for reporting the status, results, and values of EPIs to consumers, stockholders, and regulatory agencies, among others.

Why is the IT department so able to be of benefit during the assessment stage? The IT department is no stranger to enterprise- and organization-wide projects, enterprise reporting, audits, and the use of metrics to manage itself; it also offers these capabilities to the rest of the organization. The IT department is continuously engaged in many data visualization projects that are used throughout the organization to assess business functions. IT department resources are experienced with organizational assessment processes and practices by virtue of the role definition and their daily interaction with the business.

The assessment stage is the culmination of different component, processes, tools, resources, and much more. To generalize the stage with the aid of a formula, Figure 6.1 offers a graphic depiction. The formula, also depicted in text form, relates reporting, tracking, auditing, and surveying with the addition of IT department

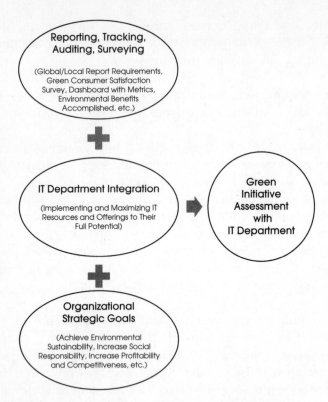

Figure 6.1   Formula for Green Initiative Assessment with IT Department

integration and organizational strategic goals as components for Green initiative assessment with the IT department.

Reporting, Tracking, Auditing, Surveying + IT Department Integration + Organizational Strategic Goals = Green Initiative Assessment with IT department

The formula shows the importance of the IT department integration; not having this integration would hinder the organization's ability to achieve effective and productive Green initiative assessments. For an organization not to utilize its IT department's resources and offerings in an integrated manner would be a mistake.

Assessment stage processes are a culmination of steps, procedures, and practices that need to be followed in a systematic and disciplined manner. They range from Green initiative assessment team formation and utilization, IT resource and offering assignment, reporting, and much more. The next sections provide a framework and flow processes that could be used within an organization.

Assessment Stage Process Flow

As Green initiative projects are completed, the assessment stage evaluates the outcomes, benefits, and accomplishments with respect to the each objective relating to the goals of the organization (i.e., become environmentally sustainable, increase social responsibility, increase profitability, increase competitiveness, open new markets, etc.). The assessment stage includes functions of auditing, reporting, and tracking. Within this stage, the IT department contributes and participates to assist in these functions.

Green Initiative Objective Assessment

The process of analyzing Green initiative objectives with assessment criteria to determine the initiative's level of success, failure, and compliance. Methods of data collection, surveys, audits, and inspections are used to prepare for outcome analysis. Reports are used to make assessment analysis viewable to internal and external entities and allow for determination of use of outcome results.

The IT department's contribution in this stage will be similar to its contributions in other stages (i.e., utilization of its technical and human resources along with its systems, databases, and application development capabilities). During this stage, the tools and offerings that relate to surveying, tracking, auditing, and reporting are of great value and support the assessment process. The assessment stage process flow, shown in Figure 6.2, is a combination of systematic processes that take place serially but should be flexible, adaptable, and collaborative, as are other business processes that are implemented by organizations.

Many organizations need to answer the next questions before and during the assessment stage:

• How will the organization assess Green initiative effort processes, deliverables, and performance? The organization must

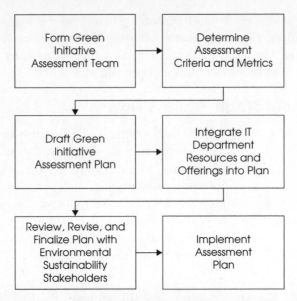

Figure 6.2   Implementation Phase Process Flow with IT Department

continue to assess value after the tasks and milestones are complete. This is when the promised benefits of the effort are finally realized or are identified as falling short.

- What is the organization's definition and processes regarding postproject evaluation? What priority, resources, and efforts are to be applied to assessing Green initiative efforts? If this assessment will be of low priority and effort, the organization may want to reconsider this level of priority. The work you put in to this effort will be reflected in what you get out.

- What has been the level of complexity, ease, and effectiveness of prior postinitiative assessments? If the complexity was high and the ease of use and effectiveness was low, it is time to reevaluate the assessment process before using it with Green initiative efforts. Postinitiative assessment need not be complex to be effective. With time to market and the need to comply with regulatory compliances, there is not much time available for lengthy postinitiative assessments.

- What is the time between the start of a postinitiative assessment and the end of the initiative it is assessing? A postinitiative quality assessment can occur within days, weeks, and even months of the validated completion. What effect will assessment delay have on the assessment's effectiveness and value to the organization? Will stakeholders accept delays in the assessment? Will the delay reduce the benefit of applying what has been learned in the assessment to contiguous efforts within the organization, or will it not be applied?

- What types of trend analysis will be implemented during the assessment process to validate existing trends or to identify new ones? Trends may offer some concepts and areas to be aware of, look out for, and emphasize before and during the assessment process.
- How much time is allotted to assessing the actual benefits of the Green initiatives within the organization? It may take a considerable amount of time. Nevertheless, the assessment stage must offer some mechanism to evaluate the types, amount, and level of strategic benefits the organization received from the initiative (e.g., increased revenue; higher efficiencies; increased customer satisfaction). Some strategic benefits may be assessed by financial calculations or customer surveys. This effort may require some type of quantitative and/or qualitative research processes.

Some key components of the assessment stage process flow are the creation of a Green initiative assessment team, determining assessment criteria and metrics, and drafting and finalizing the assessment plan. Some of these components continue from and are similar to those used in other stages, but the uniqueness of the assessment plan requires unique research tools and processes, along with the continued integration of the IT department is repetitive and enhanced.

Green Initiative Assessment Team

The assessment stage will need a strong, professional, and collaborative team to complete the tasks of this stage. A leader will be assigned to the assessment functions, along with a supporting staff of professionals from throughout the organization to cover many of its business functions, both internal and external.

Leading an assessment effort can be challenging, overwhelming at times, and confrontational. Sometimes the leader must report bad news back to stakeholders and other corporate executives.

Thus, the assessment stage leader should have some of the next characteristics:

- Prior Green postinitiative assessment experience
- Auditing, tracking, and reporting how projects and initiatives can strategically benefit an organization
- People friendly (spending a considerable amount of time in communicating to make sure resources are available to do the work and know what work needs to be completed)
- External reporting experience relating to environmental regulatory compliance and global reporting initiatives
- Stakeholder management skills in order to effectively communicate, report to, and deal with stakeholder expectations and issues
- Planning, managing, and controlling work efforts of the assessment stage
- Allocating resources
- Defining tasks
- Assigning responsibility
- Controlling and monitoring quality
- Scrutinizing progress
- Checking performance of assigned tasks
- Appointing secondary leaders
- Building and upholding team sprit
- Setting standards and maintaining organization assessment best practices
- Training the team

Figure 6.3 depicts additional key members of the Green initiative assessment team. This team, depending on the organization's business activities (i.e., global, regional, local) can contain one or more geographically displaced subteams. Teams throughout the areas of business operations work on that area's specific regulatory compliances, environmental impacts, product and service markets, and customers. Furthermore, subteams can play an important role in the productivity and effectiveness of the team by adding depth and breadth of business knowledge, cross-business function exposure, and business relationships. Team members should have prior organization strategic assessment exposure, be team players, collaborate effectively, be respected among departments and peers, and

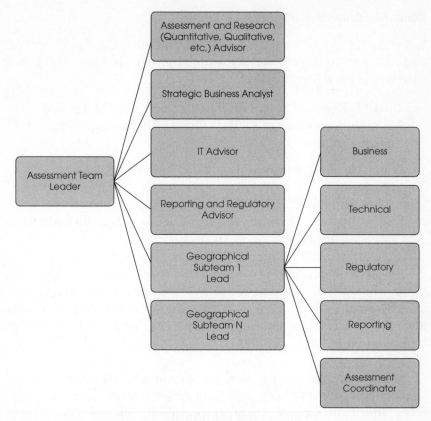

Figure 6.3   Assessment Team Organization Chart

be driven to complete assessment efforts on time. A Green initiative assessment team fulfills these key roles:

- Assessment advisor
- Strategic business analyst
- IT advisor
- Reporting and regulatory advisor
- Subteam business analysts
- Subteam technical representatives (IT, Green-related technologies, etc.)
- Subteam reporting representative
- Subteam regulatory representative
- Subteam assessment coordinator

Objective Criteria and Metrics

Let's take the first objective of a goal that was mentioned in Chapter 4 and create measurable criteria for the objective's actions. The goal's structure is presented next.

> **Goal #1: Reduce Overall IT Data Center Power Usage and Increase Percentage of IT Data Center Alternative Energy Source Usage**
>
> Objective #1: Conserve Energy Used by Servers
> - Actions:
>   - Purchase ENERGY STAR 5.0 servers.
>   - Reduce physical server count via server virtualization technology.

To establish performance criteria that relate to the strategic goals of an organization, there needs to be a set of questions that can be used systematically in assisting with criteria definition and acceptance. Some questions that organizations can ask when creating the criteria are listed next.

- What are the organization's minimum criteria for its environmental sustainability goal with respect to the areas of regulatory compliance, social responsibility, increases in market share and profitability, and customer satisfaction levels?
- How will the organization know it has met its overall environmental sustainability goal and, at a more granular level, be able to define the level of success per Green initiative effort? Will the criteria be the same for each Green initiative effort?
- How will the organization know what level of customer satisfaction comes from a specific Green initiative effort, a combination of them, or none at all?
- How will each particular Green initiative deliverable be stated as completed, completed satisfactorily, and of strategic value to the organization?

Additionally, how would the organization weigh each component of the environmental sustainability goal? For example, if the criteria of the regulatory compliance component was for the organization to be 100% compliant with regional, national, and international regulations, but other areas of the environmental sustainability goal were not met, what would be the outcome of the organization's view of meeting its environmental goal? Would one component weigh more in the decision than others?

In addition to the weight factor assigned as criteria, these factors may have to be considered:

- Timeline and/or time period
- Measurable metric
- Specifics

Now let's take the objective, "Conserve energy used by servers," shown in Table 6.1, and associate some criteria and a measurable metric to it.

Ensure that the criteria and the measurable metric are of value, and relevance to the organization, and are in alignment with the achievement of environmental sustainability within the organization.

Often, criteria are arbitrary, ambiguous, and vague, lack specificity, and cannot be measured. Examples of criteria that are not of value to the assessment process include:

- Purchase ENERGY STAR 5.0 complaint servers
- Reduce server count in data center
- Create an energy consumption reduction plan
- Hire an energy consultant

Table 6.1   Measureable Criteria Assignment

Objective	Action	Criteria	Measurable Metric
Conserve energy used by servers	Purchase ENERGY STAR 5.0 servers	Start date of FY2011 with 100% purchase compliance throughout year	FY2011 purchase order compliance %
	Reduce physical server count via server virtualization technology	Start date of FY2011 with 10% reduction by year end	FY2010 versus FY2011 physical server count

These criteria are missing measurable values: a time period, a percentage value, quantity, statistical value, and the like. Without these, establishing a measurable metric is very difficult. When establishing criteria and measurable metrics, keep in mind a performance scorecard within a dashboard that has KPIs, performance indicators (red/green/yellow lights, etc.) and thresholds. These are applicable to the scorecard because each KPI is associated with a measureable metric.

Draft Green Initiative Assessment Plan

Green initiative assessment plans need to be framed as to meet the requirements of the assessment process that is to be completed. The plan will have defined processes, shown in Figure 6.4 (i.e., assessment requirements, methods of assessing environmental objectives, applying assessment criteria to the objectives outcome and reporting the results to stakeholders, and applying these results to future Green initiative efforts to improve on their results).

Create Assessment Goals   The assessment will need to have specific goals to achieve. These goals will act as the guidelines for and

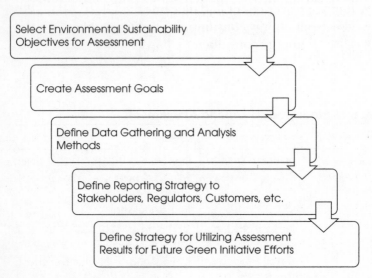

Figure 6.4   Assessment Plan Flow

focus of the assessment. Sample Green initiative–related assessment goals include:

- Start with adequate funding, executive-level support, stakeholders, and other required organizational support and acknowledgment.
- Perform assessment within determined timeline and budget.
- Encompass all areas of information gathering (qualitative and quantitative) and analysis in relation to decision making and the management of the Green initiatives and environmental sustainability.
- The four major areas of assessment will be: environmental sustainability strategic goal benefit, regulatory compliance, social responsibility, and customer satisfaction.
- Assessment will attempt to measure Green initiative progress and accomplishment with customer and stakeholder expectations and the organization's strategic goals and mission.
- Assessment efforts will have a compelling motivation, a rigorous and valid research process, and a commitment to engaging and applying the information gathered.

After the assessment goals are defined, we can take the objectives used earlier in the chapter and define intended outcomes. But before we do this, let's look at some concepts of assessment outcomes. Outcomes can be specific or general, and can relate to performance of an individual, unit, organization, or product service. Depending on the target for the outcome, different types of outcomes can be implemented (i.e., business process, application, product, service). With respect to the sample objective in Table 6.2, business performance management practices were utilized to create the intended outcomes.

Performance management processes and the organization's strategic plan are used to assist performance assessments that define intended outcomes with strategic purposes for the organization. Intended outcomes allow for verification of the success of Green initiatives in conjunction with the overall organizational strategic goal of environmental sustainability. The ability to take the outcomes of the assessment and apply the results in future Green initiative efforts is a method to help improve future organizational strategic performance levels.

Table 6.2   Intended Outcome Definition

Objective	Action	Criteria	Measurable Metric	Intended Outcome
Conserve energy used by servers	Purchase ENERGY STAR 5.0 servers	Start date of FY2011 with 100% purchase compliance throughout year	FY2011 purchase order compliance %	Organization will conserve energy used by servers by purchasing 100% ENERGY STAR 5.0 – compliant servers in 2011
	Reduce physical server count via server virtualization technology	Start Date of FY2011 with 10% reduction by year end	FY2010 vs. FY2011 physical server count	Organization will reduce physical server count via server virtualization technology by 10% in 2011

Define Data Gathering and Analysis Assessment Methods   Many data-gathering methods and techniques are available for a Green initiative assessment process. They range from surveys, interviews, inspections and data abstracts, and ad hoc querying, to imports from organizational data sources.

But before any of the data collection processes occur, let's review some dos and don'ts that should become best practices.

- **Involve the IT department.** Utilize the department from beginning to end, involve in acquiring access, tools, and extracts
- **Involve business analysts and subject matter experts (SMEs).** Gain insight into data sources through experts.
- **Document** all sources, contacts, tools, processes, and procedures of the data collection efforts.
- **Implement data integrity checks.** Verify integrity of data in source systems, extracts, and survey data.
- **Implement data validity checks.** Validate data values in sources systems, extracts against source systems, and survey data.
- **Avoid information bias.** Try to ensure that data and information are received from a cross-section of the target population that surveys and interviews are working with. This is pertinent with interviews for how questions are asked in regard to voice,

tone, body language, and setting. The attitude of interviewees may affect the way questions are asked and answers recorded. Undertake careful training to minimize the influence of these factors. Interviewers should be carefully selected and trained and given clear guidelines on how to conduct their interviews.

- **Ensure a representative sample.** They should reflect the population in general—by sex, age, consumer type, and so on.
- **Don't rely on only one source**. Obtain information as widely as possible to help avoid information bias. Strive to utilize as many tools as possible to reach out to the largest base of source information.
- **Respect confidentiality.** Respect the confidentiality of the target population. Trust and respect during the data collection process are crucial to the overall professionalism of the assessment effort. Participants may have to supply informed consent. Additionally, be clear in communicating your assessment efforts in order to reduce ambiguity and not violate trust and privacy.

Let's look closer at the survey as an assessment data collection tool. The survey will need a framework within which to work. The framework lists who is to be surveyed, the type of survey, number of questions, desired form for answers, logistical requirements and constraints, and place where the survey is to be taken.

Survey software packages are available to assist in the definition and creation of surveys. The IT department can assist with selecting, installing, and administering these surveys. *CEOWORLD* magazine published a listing in January 2010 of the Top Best Survey Software for your Business.[1]

Before selecting a survey software tool, first create a list of requirements that your Green initiative assessment surveys will need from the software so your organization can use it when talking with vendors. A sample is presented next.

- Effective online and built-in help
- Effective user manual
- Effective product support
- Competitive pricing
- Sample survey
- Survey templates
- Foreign language support
- Survey design tools that offer ease of use

IT Toolkit.com: Survey Software Example

The Project Review Survey Kit from IT Toolkit.com can enhance the experience of survey implementation:

> To make the most of any time spent reviewing project results and performance, you need to examine projects at multiple levels, starting at the big picture, and digging down to find details, contradictions and explanations. This Kit gives you the steps and tools you need to plan comprehensive post-project reviews, quickly collect feedback from multiple sources via electronic survey forms, and then analyze that feedback for "lessons learned."

- Learn how to plan an effective survey process, assigning tasks, roles and responsibilities.
- Prepare survey forms to suit project needs, collecting data from both customers and project team participants.
- Evaluate survey results to uncover valuable lessons learned.
- Prepare documented lessons and learned conclusions, and use them to improve future project performance.

Source: www.ittoolkit.com/project_review_survey.html

- Deployment to Web sites in different formats (i.e., HTML, XML, etc.)
- Built-in customization and/or ad hoc reporting of survey data
- Data collection
- Create single- and multiple-page Web surveys
- Online surveys support passwords, branching, and validity checking
- Store respondents' answers in a file on your server or have them e-mailed to you
- Merge information from an existing data base with respondents' answers to a survey
- Accommodate multiple variable type and question formats
- Spell checkers for survey questions and data collected
- Offered in multiple languages
- Automatic backup of survey forms and data

- Interviewing and manual data entry
- Form-based data manager with validity checking and double-entry verification
- Comprehensive selection of statistical procedures
- Custom-designed statistical analysis tables and graphics
- Data import and export capabilities (i.e., export the data to Microsoft Access or a tab- or comma-delimited text file)
- Data batch processing that is interactive, Graphical User Interface (GUI) and command-line capable
- Data processing scheduler (i.e., automatically upload and download files to and from your server)
- Web survey module that allows for conducting online surveys and e-mail questionnaires
- Full e-mail list capture and maintenance capabilities
- Large e-mail list support (i.e., millions of names)
- Bulk e-mailer sends customized and serialized e-mail invitations
- E-mail tracking of who responded and ability to send reminder e-mails to those who did not
- Survey auditing capabilities
- Survey versioning capabilities

Inspections also can be used as data collection tools. Inspections can be viewed as an observation type of data collection. Inspection data can be from inspections that have already occurred and/or are going to occur within the assessment period. Scheduling of inspections that are going to occur within the assessment period could have been planned or created by ad hoc requirements. Additionally, the scheduling of inspections can be done independently of the assessment but can add great value to the assessment. Furthermore, inspections can be mandatory or voluntary. Inspections are visits to a facility or site (e.g., business, landfill, chemical processing plant, offshore operations) for the purpose of gathering information to determine whether it is in compliance with an environmental regulation. Regulatory inspections can be performed from within the organization or by an independent inspection agency or firm, with the government regulatory agency imposing the regulation.

Inspections can include preinspection activities, such as obtaining general site information, security clearances, and preparing data and reports, before entering the facility or site. Once onsite, a number of events can occur, some of which the inspectors may be aware of and some that may come as complete surprises. Some additional activities that may occur by inspectors that yield data and offer assistance to assessment analysis are as follows:

- Interviewing of facility or site representatives
- Reviewing of records and reports
- Taking of photographs and video
- Collecting air, soil, water, production, and processing samples
- Adding measurement and data collecting equipment to existing facilities or sites
- Observing facility or site operations

The next option for data collection is the use of interviews. Interviews are a component of the qualitative research method. There are different types of interviews. The types that would be of benefit to Green initiative assessments include evaluation, one-to-one, and focus group interviews. Evaluation interviews examine new programs and developments and suggest improvements. One-to-one interviews allow for a single interviewee to be interviewed in a setting that may be more comfortable and less threatening, thus yielding better results. In focus group interviews, people meet to share their impressions of changes in a product or an organization.

Problems with interviews arise because they allow for interviewer involvement, create the opportunity for opinions and impressions. Interviews are very resource intensive and time consuming. Additionally, the data analysis must consider the interviewer as part of the measurement instrument. There are technologies and computer software that the IT department can use to promote effective interviewing. This includes voice and video recording and interview computer software that tracks each interview's structural and collected information.

QSR International offers two software products, NVivo and XSIGHT, that assist with data collection and analysis. "If you need to handle rich information, where in-depth analysis on both small and large volumes of data are required, NVivo 8 is your solution. It removes many of the manual tasks associated with analysis, like classifying, sorting and arranging information, so you have more time to explore trends, test theories and arrive at answers to questions."[2]

After determining the method of data gathering, the data collection can begin. The data collection ability of defining data extracts, reports, and ad hoc query access to existing organizational database systems will be of value to analyze purchase orders, sales, and other transactional data. Additionally, organizations contain data repositories of historical data that is used in data warehouses and business intelligence applications. The IT department can be of assistance in gaining access to these data sources, applications, and reporting systems to aid in the data collection strategy.

After completion of data collection, the process of collating the data with respect to variables, groups, and categories begins. This sets the stage for data analysis. Define what type of analysis the assessment process will utilize. One type of analysis is identifying trends related to the benefits of the Green initiatives in relation to the accomplishment of the organization's environmental sustainability goal. The granularity of trend analysis can be from one Green initiative to the next as well as to each task completed within each Green initiative effort. Trends offer who, why, and where analysis and with the aid of data mining algorithms, the potential for how, why, and where into the near future. The IT department can assist with the selection and deployment of a data mining application that can be Web and/or desktop based (i.e., Microsoft Office Excel).

Having all of this data available for collection will require effective and productive data analysis tools, which the IT department can help users to understand and access. Other analysis methods include summarizing the data in charts, tables, and maps. Data visualization is a key component of data analysis.

Table 6.3 shows the intended outcomes, assessment methods, and expected results.

Define Reporting Strategy to Stakeholders, Regulators, and Customers This step of the assessment plan defines the reporting strategy that will meet internal and external reporting requirements of the organization, regulatory agencies, and customers. Assess current internal reporting systems for usage and applicability. Factor in the need for an additional external reporting system, costs, training, and deployment. The IT department can assist in this process.

Break the strategy down in this way:

- **Internal reports.** Internal reports allow management and other decision makers to analyze processes, procedures, products,

Table 6.3 Assessment Method

Intended Outcome	Assessment Method	Expected results
Organization will conserve energy used by servers by purchasing 100% ENERGY STAR 5.0 compliant servers in 2011.	1. Survey employees who purchase server hardware on what their participation has been in this process. What percentage of servers they purchased were compliant? If not compliant, what were the reason(s)? 2. Conduct a data extraction assessment of server hardware purchased in 2011 via purchase orders stored within organization databases. 3. Conduct a data extraction assessment of energy consumption via electric bills, payments, etc.	1. 100% ENERGY STAR 5.0–compliant server purchases in 2011. 2. Exceptions for not purchasing ENERGY STAR 5.0–compliant servers were resolved. 3. Overall reduction of energy consumption, costs, and payments in 2011.
Organization will reduce physical server count via server virtualization technology by 10% in 2011.	1. Survey data center employees who deploy and manage servers on what their participation has been in this process. What percentage of servers they deployed were virtualized? If not virtualized, what were the reason(s)? 2. Conduct a data extraction assessment of the servers deployed within 2011 via server deployment requests stored in organizational databases. 3. Conduct a data extraction assessment of overall and year 2011 server deployments with respect to physical and virtualized servers stored within the organization's databases.	1. Overall reduction in physical servers operating within data centers. 2. Increase in deployment of virtualized servers in 2011. 3. Exceptions for not deploying virtualized servers were resolved.

and services to verify benefit to the environmental sustainability strategic goal and to possibly find ways to improve on them.
- Perform assessment of internal report audience
- Different levels of needs and granularity
- Real-time needs
- Dashboards with scorecards containing performance metrics
- Accessibility requirements
- **External reports**. External-facing reporting systems and/or hard copy reports offer verification of regulatory compliances and level of social responsibility and allow for consumers to evaluate whether Greenwashing practices are used or that an organization is sincere and effective with promises and practices. An organization's report information may also be presented in a survey that creates a report across organizations and industries that is offered in government, consumer, and trade magazines and Web sites.
  - Perform assessment of external report requirements
  - Review the Global Reporting Initiative organization
  - Ask about format and content requirements
  - Data security and confidentiality challenges and concerns
  - Ask for sample reports, templates, support

Global Reporting Initiative: Reporting Example

The Global Reporting Initiative (GRI) is a network-based organization that has pioneered the development of the world's most widely used sustainability reporting framework and is committed to its continuous improvement and application worldwide. GRI is a collaborating center of the UN Environment Program, and the GRI guidelines have synergies with the UN Global Compact.

Source: www.globalreporting.org/aboutgri/whatisgri/alliances/grialliances-page.htm

Define Strategy for Utilizing Results for Future Green Initiative Improvements Once the reports of the assessment's findings have been created, the next process is to interpret the findings in a way that can create adjustments, modifications, and recommendations to improve on future Green initiative efforts. This step of the assessment stage is crucial due to its benefit to the organization. Not performing this step would prevent the organization from maximizing the capabilities of the overall assessment process.

Depending on the recommendation changes, supplemental Green initiatives may be developed that improve on prior Green initiatives, or new Green initiatives may be developed.

The strategy for utilizing results could benefit from an understanding of strategic goal management, change management, risk management, and project management processes within the organization. These areas can take the assessment results and turn them into action.

The opportunity to turn the results of the assessment into productive actions is not a formality but rather deserves ample resources, priority, and funding to complete. Finalizing the assessment does not stop at the creation of the reports and recommendations; utilization is the step.

Assign IT Resources and Offerings to the Plan

The Green initiative assessment stage can take advantage of IT department human and technical resources as well as the many offerings that the other stages (i.e., planning, implementation) relating to Green initiative efforts did. The assessment plan, requirements, duration, scope, and budget will determine the extent of the use and types of IT department resources and offerings. The assignment and selection of IT department resources and offerings is as crucial as is their utilization, maximization, and availability.

Looking at human resources, employees are the most valuable asset and the biggest expense for most organizations. Additionally, they can also be the scarcest resource. The ability to deploy employees effectively despite other conflicting organizational needs and work priorities is the challenge in assigning IT department resources. This is not to scare the assessment leader into thinking that IT department resources will not be available; it is merely a reminder that, due to the benefits of IT department resources to the organization, they are often heavily utilized. With proper and effective planning, prioritization, budgeting, and communication, IT resources can be available for the assessment stage. In order to maximize both assessment planning execution and resource assignment and utilization, the assessment team leader will need to have an efficient resource management system to assign the appropriate staff to the right task at the right time.

IT department resource demands must be viewed across the organization so the assessment team leader can make staffing decisions to support the assessment stage. This will entail communication with the IT department management to understand what types of resources are available and their role and skill sets. Let's look at the list of human and technical resources that are available for the assessment stage:

- Human Resources
  - Green IT advisors
  - Directors and managers
  - IT architects
  - System architects
  - Data center engineers
  - Database administrators
  - Network engineers
  - System analysts
  - Application developers
  - Help desk/support
- Technology Resources
  - Data centers: power, cooling, hosting
  - Networks: intranet, Internet, extranet, mobile, wireless, wired
  - Desktops/laptops
  - Servers: virtual/physical, file, print, application, database, management
  - Disk storage: storage area network (SAN), network attached storage (NAS)
  - Mobile devices: PDA, cell phones
  - Backup/restore: tape units
- Offerings
  - Green IT assessment, procurement, and advising
  - Asset management
  - Application portfolio management
  - Custom application development
  - IT-business application design and planning
  - IT systems and data center design and management
  - Enterprise data management/master data management
  - Tactical, operational, and strategic reporting

- Business intelligence analytics and predictive analysis
- Business performance management
- Auditing and regulatory compliance

The assessment stage emphasizes data collection, analysis, and reporting. Understanding this fact can assist with determining which subset of resources from the list is of value at this time. Examples of IT resources and offerings would be database administrators, application development that was relative to report development, business intelligence analytics and predictive analysis that offered data mining, and business performance management that offered dashboard and scorecards with performance metrics, and so on.

Finalize Green Initiative Assessment Plan

Finalizing the Green Initiative assessment plan with stakeholders and others should be an official process that implements sign-off and acceptance and tracks the results of the assessment. This finalization process could expose organizational politics, hidden agendas, negative influences, and the act of torpedoing the assessment plan, and much more. Keep in mind that one or more stakeholders may have a negative view on the organization's Green initiative efforts and the results. This fact should be taken into consideration by the assessment leader and others on the assessment team every time you interact with stakeholders and ask for feedback and approval. Effective stakeholder management and the ability to identify negative and deceptive characteristics, actions, and tactics are key for the assessment leader and team.

Furthermore, with assessments related to environmental sustainability, other internal and external entities could pose a challenge to the approval of the assessment due to data collection, analysis, reporting, and results. (These challenges could include disruptions in funding for the assessment stage, reprioritization of the stage, regulatory inspections, consumer sentiment reflected in surveys due to shifts in consumer demands, sudden disruption in the organization's special responsibility and ethical practices and image, instability in local and global economies, geopolitical events, and the like.) It will take a skilled assessment leader to deal with all of these issues and challenges and find ways to head them off and deal with them to turn them into positives.

Finalization of the assessment plan allows for the next step to occur: implementation.

Implement Green Initiative Assessment Plan

The execution of the Green initiative assessment plan typically is the longest part of the assessment stage. The assessment stage could continue for years, depending on the scope, budget, goals, and how many outcomes are to be assessed. Furthermore, implementation consumes the majority of resources allocated to the assessment stage, including time, people, equipment, and budget. With this in mind, it is essential assessment plan implementation be managed effectively and in a way that continues to motivate, collaborate, and show value to the organization. Otherwise, it could be viewed as a money pit that is consuming extremely valuable resources but offers no strategic value.

Data Collection   The data collection process implements the surveys, inspections, and interviews that were defined within the plan. Doing this requires that the surveys be developed and the collection of entered data placed online. Surveys are created using the tool determined in the assessment plan and are offered to the target population for each survey.

The inspection process is twofold: scheduling new inspections and utilizing past inspections. The scheduling of new inspections is determined by the regulatory agency participating in the inspection, organizational resource availability, dependencies, criteria for starting the inspection, and much more. Nevertheless, it is crucial that these inspections are accomplished and completed effectively so that the regulatory agency can make a productive assessment via the inspection results, as to give the organization feedback that can assist in the best chance in achieving compliance.

Interview personnel will need to be mobilized. This will require scheduling of interviews, implementing the defined interview style and technique defined within the plan, and gathering data. The computer software application selected in the assessment plan will be used in managing and collecting of unstructured data. If interviews have many different types of data formats (i.e., notes, videos, voice recordings, etc.), computer software will be required to structure the unstructured data so analysis can be done effectively.

The data collected via data abstracts and ad hoc query access to organizational data sources can be passed on to data analysis processing. Doing this should involve the IT department, business analyst, and computer systems analyst to determine access and data sets from the data sources for the assessment's needs. Furthermore, an assessment stage data repository may be created to hold the data obtained from extracts, imports, and ad hoc queries that can be integrated with data obtained in other ways.

Data Analysis Data analysis takes the data collected from all the collection tools, processes, and repositories and implements the data analysis procedures defined within the assessment plan. Powerful computer software applications, implemented by the IT department, are required to complete the data analysis tasks. The end result is the ability to complete the column in Table 6.4 labeled "Actual Results."

The actual results are based on the data analysis processes, assessment method selection and criteria, expected result values and ranges, and interpretations of the assessment team. From here, the results go to the stakeholders for review. Some additional interpretation of the actual results could lead to conflicts, changes, or deviations. Nevertheless, the actual results will have to be finalized and documented, even if not everyone likes and agrees on them.

Ethical rules are critical in the data analysis process. Furthermore, bias and hidden agendas have to be monitored and managed. The need to reduce human interpretations and allow for exact matching and determination of actual results via quantitative criteria may reduce the effects of bias and hidden agendas.

Utilize Results for Future Green Initiative Improvements Assessment results are of utmost value when shared with team members, stakeholders, customers, and regulatory agencies. They are tools for facilitating discussion about improving future Green initiative efforts. These efforts may be to go back to a completed Green initiative and improve on it or begin entirely new Green initiative efforts. The use of the assessment results are defined within the assessment plan and are to be reviewed via collaborative processes that get the results to the appropriate internal and external organizational business operational area(s).

Table 6.4 Actual Results Analysis

Intended Outcome	Assessment Method	Expected Results	Actual Results
Organization will conserve energy used by servers by purchasing 100% ENERGY STAR 5.0 compliant servers in 2011.	1. Survey employees who purchase server hardware on what their participation has been in this process. What percentage of servers they purchased were compliant? If not compliant, what were the reason(s)? 2. Conduct a data extraction assessment of server hardware purchased in 2011 via purchase orders stored within organization databases. 3. Conduct a data extraction assessment of energy consumption via electric bills, payments, etc.	1. 100% ENERGY STAR 5.0-compliant server purchases in 2011. 2. Exceptions for not purchasing ENERGY STAR 5.0-compliant servers were resolved. 3. Overall reduction of energy consumption, costs, and payments in 2011.	1. 98% ENERGY STAR 5.0-compliant servers purchased in 2011. 2. Exceptions for 2% not being ENERGY STAR 5.0 compliant due to organizational mission-critical decisions. 3. 15% reduction in energy consumption and 10% decrease in energy costs achieved in 2011.
Organization will reduce physical server count via server virtualization technology by 10% in 2011.	1. Survey data center employees who deploy and manage servers on what their participation has been in this process. What percentage of servers they deployed were virtualized? If not virtualized, what were the reason(s)? 2. Conduct a data extraction assessment of the servers deployed within 2011 via server deployment requests stored in organizational databases. 3. Conduct a data extraction assessment of overall and year 2011 server deployments with respect to physical and virtualized servers stored within the organization's databases.	1. Overall reduction in physical servers operating within data centers. 2. Increase in deployment of virtualized servers in 2011. 3. Exceptions for not deploying virtualized servers were resolved.	1. 12% reduction in overall number of physical servers operating in data centers at year-end 2011. 2. Virtualization server deployments increased by 9% in 2011. 3. 57% of exceptions resolved.

Meetings must be scheduled to establish what assessment results are to be targeted for revision, new efforts, and enhancements relating to Green initiative efforts. Use of the results should be tracked as well (as shown in Table 6.5) with the addition of the "Use of Results" column.

Use of the results will be targeted to Green-initiative efforts and the overall organizational assessment process. Results may lead to recommendations to improve processes, assessment team membership, length of assessments, plan definition template, and much more.

Some key areas and aspects related to the use of the results are common for Green initiative efforts and general assessment practices. They are:

- Identify what was done well.
- Specify where it could have been improved.
- Discover what was learned that can be used in future projects.
- Identify improvement areas.
- Prioritize improvement areas.
- Identify a team to implement improvements.
- Create or utilize existing Centers of Excellence to use the results.
- Review quality improvement processes, standards, and best practices internally and externally.
- Manage and monitor improvements over time.

Assessment Stage Tips

A list of tips, comments, and strong recommendations is presented next.

- Assign an assessment leader with prior experience who exhibits many of the required traits and skill sets needed to perform effectively.
- Assign members to the assessment team who are representative of the organization and the overall environmental sustainability goal and also have assessment planning experiences. Include personnel from the IT department from the beginning to the end of the assessment stage.
- Utilize research methods (i.e., qualitative and quantitative) during data collection definition and implementation.

Table 6.5 Use of Results

Intended Outcome	Assessment Method	Expected Results	Actual Results	Use of Results
Organization will conserve energy used by servers by purchasing 100% ENERGY STAR 5.0 compliant servers in 2011.	1. Survey employees who purchase server hardware on what their participation has been in this process. What percentage of servers they purchased were compliant? If not compliant, what were the reason(s)? 2. Conduct a data extraction assessment of server hardware purchased in 2011 via purchase orders stored within organization databases. 3. Conduct a data extraction assessment of energy consumption via electric bills, payments, etc.	1. 100% ENERGY STAR 5.0-compliant server purchases in 2011. 2. Exceptions for not purchasing ENERGY STAR 5.0-compliant servers were resolved. 3. Overall reduction of energy consumption, costs, and payments in 2011.	1. 98% ENERGY STAR 5.0-compliant servers purchased in 2011. 2. Exceptions for 2% not being ENERGY STAR 5.0 compliant due to organizational mission-critical decisions. 3. 15% reduction in energy consumption and 10% decrease in energy costs achieved in 2011.	1. Create organization-wide standard that defines ENERGY STAR 5.0-compliant servers as the default purchase standard. 2. Have IT and other organization members form a team that participates with the EPA in new ENERGY STAR 5.0-compliant standards and updates relating to computer hardware.
Organization will reduce physical server count via server virtualization technology by 10% in 2011.	1. Survey data center employees who deploy and manage servers on what their participation has been in this process. What percentage of servers they deployed were virtualized? If not virtualized, what were the reason(s)? 2. Conduct a data extraction assessment of the servers deployed within 2011 via server deployment requests stored in organizational databases. 3. Conduct a data extraction assessment of overall and year 2011 server deployments with respect to physical and virtualized servers stored within the organization's databases.	1. Overall reduction in physical servers operating within data centers. 2. Increase in deployment of virtualized servers in 2011. 3. Exceptions for not deploying virtualized servers were resolved.	1. 12% reduction in overall number of physical servers operating in data centers at year-end 2011. 2. Virtualization server deployments increased by 9% in 2011. 3. 57% of exceptions resolved.	1. Create organization-wide standard that defines reduction of physical servers via the use of server virtualization as a best practice and part of the Center of Excellence charter.

- Review the use of survey software with the IT department for its benefits in the assessment stage.
- Creating a plan that the organization can manage and sustain is essential. Focus on only one or two outcomes at a time. Pick the outcomes that are most important to the organization and assess them first.
- Utilize and integrate the IT department as to maximize its resources and offerings (i.e., data collection and data analysis experience and offerings).
- Be sure to include sufficient time for each step of the assessment plan. Allow for enough time to complete all of the assessment steps.
- Keep in mind that the purpose of assessment is to improve Green initiatives. Focussing on this goal can help the assessment team and organization stay motivated.

Summary

Green initiative assessment with the IT department is the last stage and one that requires as much or possibly more attention, budgeting, organizational support, and sponsorship than the other stages. This is due to the value that the assessment stage brings to completing a Green initiative effort. This stage offers insight into how to effectively assess the organization's Green initiatives with respect to achieving environmental sustainability and other strategic goals related to enhancing social responsibility, improving customer satisfaction, and increasing competiveness. This is all possible with the aid of the IT department's resources and offerings that are utilized within the assessment stage.

The assessment process encompasses the creation of an assessment plan, forming an assessment team, finalizing the plan, integrating IT resources and offerings, and implementing the plan. Data collection is implemented to support the assessment process and can be performed via surveys, inspections, and interviews. It can utilize existing organizational data sources via ad hoc reports, extracts, and the like.

Performance management processes and tools from the IT department can be used in the assessment stage to monitor performance indicators related to Green initiative results and expectations. Dashboards with balanced scorecards displaying key performance indicators can offer effective and productive data visualization that displays metrics related to the goal objective's assessment criteria. External reports for regulatory compliance also can be produced.

Knowing how well each Green initiative effort has benefited the organization will aid in determining how to use the assessment results in a productive manner to plan for updates and modifications to new processes.

Notes

1. http://ceoworld.biz/ceo/2010/01/25/top-best-survey-software-for-your-business
2. www.qsrinternational.com/products_nvivo.aspx

Appendix A

RESOURCES AND LINKS

Associations, Research, Certification

Gartner, Inc.: www.gartner.com/technology/home.jsp

Green Grid: www.thegreengrid.org/

Green Technology Alliance: www.greentechnologyalliance.org/gta/

EPEAT: www.epeat.net/default.aspx

Technology Business Research, Inc.: www.tbri.com/news/press releases.cfm

EcoLableing.org: http://ecolabelling.org/

Project Management Institute: www.pmi.org/Pages/default.aspx

Worldwide Institute: www.worldwatch.org/

World Environment Center: www.wec.org/

International Society for Performance Improvement (ISPI): www.ispi.org/

Corporate Social Responsibility Newswire (CSRwire): www.csrwire.com

International Organization for Standardization (ISO): www.iso.org/iso/iso_14000_essentials

Books and Magazines

Our Choice: A Plan to Solve the Climate Crisis, by Al Gore

CIO magazine: www.cio.com/

CEOWorld magazine: http://ceoworld.biz/ceo/

Government

United States Environmental Protection Agency (EPA): www.epa.gov

American Recovery and Reinvestment Act of 2009: www.epa.gov/recovery/

ENERGY STAR Web site allows for searching of ENERGY STAR-labeled notebooks/laptops: www.energystar.gov/index.cfm?fuseaction=find_a_product.showProductGroup&pgw_code=LT

United States EPA Design for Environment: www.epa.gov/dfe/

United States White House Energy & Environment: www.whitehouse.gov/issues/energy_and_environment

European Commission Environment: http://ec.europa.eu/environment/index_en.htm

European Union Waste Electrical and Electronic Equipment (WEEE) Directive: http://ec.europa.eu/environment/waste/weee/index_en.htm

United Nations Environment Programme (UNEP): www.unep.org/

United Nations Framework Convention on Climate Change (UNFCCC): www.unep.org/climatechange/

IT and Computer Vendors

Microsoft Virtualization: www.microsoft.com/virtualization/default.mspx

Microsoft Environment: www.microsoft.com/environment

Microsoft Dynamics AX Environmental Dashboard: www.microsoft.com/environment/business_solutions/articles/dynamics_ax.aspx www.microsoft.com/dynamics/en/us/environment.aspx

Microsoft Project 2010: www.microsoft.com/project/en/us/default.aspx

Microsoft Hohm: www.microsoft-hohm.com

SAS for Sustainability Management: www.sas.com/solutions/sustainability/

Hewlett Packard ECO Solutions: www.hp.com/hpinfo/globalcitizenship/environment/

Dell Earth: http://content.dell.com/us/en/corp/dell-earth.aspx

Intel Corporation: www.intel.com/intel/other/ehs/iso.htm

Appendix B

PLANNING GREEN INITIATIVES WITH IT CHECKLIST

This checklist can serve as a template for Green initiative planning topics that encompass a typical planning stage. Having such a checklist available can expedite Green initiative planning efforts.

Item #	Planning Topic	Comment	Status	Status Date
1	**Implement Environmental Management System (EMS)**			
	ISO 14001:2004	ISO Standard for EMS		
	Assess Current Environmental Systems as Candidates for Integration, Migration, etc.	Work with IT department via application portfolio listings, Environmental Information Management Systems, Geographic Information Systems, etc.		
	Utilize Continuous Improvement Cycle	Commitment and policy, planning, implementation, evaluation, review.		
2	**Form Environmental Sustainability Steering Committee**			
	Executive Sponsors and Membership	CEO, CIO, sustainability officer, etc.		
	Mission Statement			

(Continued)

(Continued)

Item #	Planning Topic	Comment	Status	Status Date
	Portal Site for Collaboration			
	Meeting Frequency			
3	**Create Task Forces**			
	Choose Types			
	Mission Statement			
	Portal Site for Collaboration			
	Feedback Process to Steering Committee			
4	**Establish Baseline Environmental Sustainability Data**			
	Determine Areas to Be Assessed	Water and electricity usage, hazardous materials, regulatory compliance, etc.		
	Informational and Data Sources	Transactional data warehouse, reporting, etc. Work with IT department to gain access and with business analysts to gain understanding of systems.		
	Collect Data	Extract, Transform, and Load (ETL), source system analysis, subject matter experts, etc. Engage with IT department, developers, and other personnel to work with data sets, extracts, etc.		

Item #	Planning Topic	Comment	Status	Status Date
	Collaborate with Steering Committee	Meetings, portal, etc. Work with IT on creating and setting up a collaborative portal on the intranet.		
	Create and Finalize Baseline Data Environmental Assessment (EA)			
5	**Define Environmental Aspects and Impacts**			
	Ensure EMS Is Utilized			
	Refer to Baseline Data EA	For assistance in aspect and impact analysis.		
	Determine Core Operations and Supporting Activities	Based on both products and services, where applicable.		
	Construct Input/Process/ Output Diagrams	Utilize process-mapping software to establish environmental relevance (i.e. disposal of chemicals, use of recyclable material in production, etc.) within defined processes.		
	Identify Environmental Aspects and Impacts from Process Maps	Should have influence and be controllable (consumption of electricity) by organization; do not select aspects that are outside the organization's control (electrical generation). Can be positive or negative on environment		

(Continued)

(Continued)

Item #	Planning Topic	Comment	Status	Status Date
	Develop a List or Matrix of Environmental Aspects and Impacts			
	Prioritize Environmental Aspects Based on Approved Criteria and Processes			
6	**Create Environmental Sustainability Goals and Objectives**			
	Short-Term Goals			
	Long-Term Goals			
	Statement			
	Definition			
	Scope and Timeline			
	Assumptions			
	Constraints			
	Achievability Reference			
	Organizational Resources Required			
	Training and Awareness Needs			
	Risk Analysis			
	Integrate IT Resources and Offerings			
7	**Revise Plan with Task Force Input and Steering Committee Leadership**			
	Change Control Process	Official process of reviewing, implementing, approving, and managing changes to the plan.		

(Continued)

Item #	Planning Topic	Comment	Status	Status Date
	Impact Analysis	What will be the net effect of the change (i.e., social, economic, political, environmental, business, costs, regulatory)?		
	Risk Analysis	What is the risk to the organization and environment to move forward or not, and on what timeline with the change?		
	Cost Differential Analysis	What is the cost to the organization if the changes are implemented in comparison with the original projected plan budget?		

Appendix C
IMPLEMENTING GREEN INITIATIVES WITH IT CHECKLIST

This checklist can serve as a template and implementation-stage starting point that offers examples of Green initiative topics that encompass a typical implementation stage. Such a checklist available can expedite Green initiative implementation efforts.

Item #	Planning Topic	Comment	Status	Status Date
1	**Retrieve Environmental Sustainability Goals and Objectives from EMS**			
2	**Form Green Initiative Project Management Team(s)**			
	Project Management Office (PMO)	Department or group that defines and maintains the standards and processes related to project management within an organization.		
	Project Manager			
	IT Department Environmental Sustainability Lead			
	Business Environmental Sustainability Lead			

(Continued)

(Continued)

Item #	Planning Topic	Comment	Status	Status Date
	Legal and Regulatory Representative			
	Environmental Sustainability Steering Committee Representative			
	Finance and Budget Representative			
	Environmental Sustainability Partnership and Alliances Representative			
3	**Draft Green Initiative Project Plans**			
	Define and Document the Structure, Procedures, and Processes of Project Management Up Front.			
	Project Definition and Work Plan			
	Tracking, Auditing, Reporting			
	Tools and Applications			
	Dependency Management			
	Human and Technical Resource Requirements			
	Risk and Control Management			
	Communication Plan			
4	**Assign IT Resources and Offerings**			
	Human Resources			
	Technical Resources			

Item #	Planning Topic	Comment	Status	Status Date
	Offerings			
	Homeshoring, Offshoring, Nearshoring			
5	**Review, Revise, and Finalize Green Initiative Project Plans with Stakeholders**			
	Stakeholder Management			
	Obtain Feedback	Project status, funding, deliverables.		
	Offer Workshops	Project dashboard usage, performance indicators, scorecard, reports, etc.		
	Offer Demonstrations of Deliverables			
	Change Control Process	Manage changes to project scope, funding, timelines, etc.		
	Finalize Project Plan Process	Official sign-off and approval process.		
6	**Implement Project Plans**			
	Project Status Report Usage			
	Invoke Communication Plan			
	Deliverables			
	Deliverable Requirement	Create deliverables based on requirements		
	Quality Control	Invoke a deliverable quality control process to validate quality and validity of deliverables		

(Continued)

(Continued)

Item #	Planning Topic	Comment	Status	Status Date
7	**Manage, Monitor, and Measure**			
	Manage the Work Plan			
	Monitor the Schedule			
	Monitor the Budget			
	Monitor the Warning Signs			
	Manage the Project Scope			
	Manage the Risks			
	Manage Conflicts			
	Measure Progress			

Glossary

achievement (status) An update of a plan that takes account of the progress of the tasks/projects and the changes in their duration.

bio-based product A product (other than food or feed) that is produced from renewable, agricultural (plant, animal, and marine), or forestry materials.

biodegradable A product or material capable of decomposing in nature within a reasonably short period of time.

business performance management (BPM) A continuous process of identifying, measuring, and developing the performance of individuals and teams and aligning it with the strategic goals of the organization.

carbon footprint The total amount of greenhouse gases emitted directly or indirectly through an activity or from a product, company, or person, typically expressed in equivalent tons of either carbon or carbon dioxide (CO_2). A carbon footprint is the measure of the environmental impact of a particular individual or organization's lifestyle or operation, measured in units of CO_2.

carbon neutral Effectively means net zero carbon emissions to the atmosphere. Achieving carbon neutrality means measuring the carbon emissions for an identified product, service, or company, then balancing those emissions with carbon reductions or carbon offsets to reach net zero carbon emissions. To be carbon neutral is to balance the amount of carbon dioxide released into the atmosphere by a particular activity (i.e. operating an IT data center, computer equipment manufacturing, etc.) with an equal amount of carbon sequestration or carbon offsets from a third party. To be considered carbon neutral, an individual or organization must reduce its carbon footprint to zero.

carbon offset   A credit that an individual or organization can purchase to negate a carbon footprint, thereby achieving carbon neutrality. Revenue generated from the purchase of offsets typically is invested in environmentally friendly projects. The sale of carbon offsets is a fast-growing industry in the wake of compliance legislation and the development of cap-and-trade systems.

cap-and-trade system   Market-based approach to controlling pollution that allows corporations or national governments to trade emissions allowances under an overall cap, or limit, on those emissions. Examples are the European Union Emission Trading Scheme (or EU ETS), the Australian Trading Scheme, and the Western Climate Initiative.

carbon sequestration   Biological, chemical, or physical processes used to mitigate the accumulation of greenhouse gases in the atmosphere via the long-term storage of carbon dioxide (CO_2) or other forms of carbon, for the mitigation of global warming. Trees can be used for carbon sequestration because they absorb (CO_2), release the oxygen, and store the carbon.

CGO/CSO   A CGO is a chief Green officer. A CGO is tasked with all aspects of making an organization Greener, including energy-efficient construction, e-cycling and e-waste mitigation, recycling, LEED (Leadership in Energy and Environmental Design) compliance, OSHA (Occupational Safety & Health Administration) standards and clean production, if applicable. Another title might be chief sustainability officer (CSO).

clean computing   When an organization's manufacture, use, and disposal of IT equipment do not produce any harmful waste at any stage (i.e., non-hazardous materials are used in chip construction and packaging).

climate change   A change in the "average weather" that a given region experiences. When we speak of climate change on a global scale, we are referring to changes in the climate of Earth as a whole, including temperature increases (global warming) or decreases, and shifts in wind.

closed-loop recycling   The process of utilizing a recycled product in the manufacturing of a similar product or the remanufacturing of the same product.

cloud computing   A style of computing that utilizes Internet- ("cloud-") based development and the use of computer technology where massively scalable and virtualized IT-related capabilities are provided "as a service" to multiple external customers using Internet technologies.

data center infrastructure efficiency (DCIE)   A metric used to determine the energy efficiency of a data center. Like power usage effectiveness (PUE), the reciprocal of DCIE, the metric is calculated by dividing the amount of power entering a facility to the amount of power used by the equipment within it. Unlike PUE, DCIE is expressed as a percentage. A data center's DCIE therefore improves as it approaches 100%. The metric was created by members of The Green Grid.

deliverable   Work to be delivered to a client or stakeholder that has been defined in the project plan and is measured against deliverable quality management processes. It can be one or more items that may have contractual obligations and be related to time and content.

dependency   A chronological link between two elements of a project. Dependencies are sequential constraints used for the relative positioning of tasks, milestones, task groups, and projects.

Design for the Environment (DfE)   A philosophy applied to the design process that advocates the reduction of environmental and human health impacts through materials selection and design strategies. The U.S. Environmental Protection Agency offers a DfE partnership program. See its Web site: www.epa.gov/dfe/.

duration (actual)   The actual amount of time that a task required. This typically is supplied after estimated duration is entered and after the task has been completed.

duration (estimated)   A best estimate of the actual amount of time that the task requires. Estimation skills and processes are to be used to assist with duration estimations.

e-cycling   The practice of reusing, or distributing for reuse, electronic equipment and components rather than discarding them at the end of their life cycle. Often even nonfunctioning devices can be refurbished and resold or donated.

e-waste   Any refuse created by discarded electronic devices and components as well as substances involved in their manufacture or use. The disposal of electronics is a growing problem because electronic equipment frequently contains hazardous substances.

economizer   A mechanical device used to reduce energy consumption. Economizers are commonly used in data centers to complement or replace cooling devices, such as computer room air conditioners or chillers. When outside temperatures and humidity levels are high, an economizer may not be practical.

efficiency   The capability of a resource to achieve a task within its theoretical duration.

effort   The task duration multiplied by the number of roles required to achieve that task.

Emission Reduction Credit (ERC)/carbon offset   Represents avoided or reduced emissions often measured in tons. ERCs are generated from projects or activities that reduce or avoid emissions. A carbon offset refers to a specific type of ERC that represents an activity that avoids or reduces greenhouse gas emissions or sequesters carbon from the atmosphere.

energy efficiency   Using less energy to fulfill the same function or purpose improves energy efficiency of the function. It can be achieved by implementing a technological change or a change in behavior. Examples include better insulation with a higher R-value to reduce heating/cooling demand, compact fluorescent bulbs to replace incandescent bulbs, proper tire inflation to improve gas mileage, replacing lower miles-per-gallon (MPG) vehicles with higher MPG vehicles, carpooling, and the like.

ENERGY STAR   A joint program of the U.S. Environmental Protection Agency and the U.S. Department of Energy helping citizens save money and protect the environment through energy-efficient products and practices. The ENERGY STAR Specification for Computers offers guidance for the purchasing of ENERGY STAR–compliant desktops, laptop, monitors, and other computer-related equipment.

energy vampires   Products in the home that suck energy while not providing any useful function. This energy is sometimes called "standby power." While standby power sometimes provides useful functions such as remote control, clock displays, and timers, in other cases it is simply wasted power as a result of leaving an electronic device or power adapter plugged in. To slay the energy vampires, enable the ENERGY STAR power management settings on your computer and monitor, so they go into power save mode when not in use; use a power strip as a central turn-off point when you are done using equipment, which completely disconnects the power supply; and unplug your chargers: cell phone chargers, camera chargers, battery chargers, or power adapters.

environmental aspect   Element of an activity, product, or service of a company that is causing or can cause an environmental impact.

environmental impact Actual interaction with or impact on the environment.

Environmentally Preferable Products (EPP) Products or services that "have a lesser or reduced effect on human health and the environment when compared with competing products or services that serve the same purpose." EPP Certification is a process by which products or services are certified as Environmentally Preferred Products. The certification addresses all stages of the product's/service's life cycle, incorporates key environmental and human health issues relevant to the category, and undergoes outside stakeholder review.

environmental performance indicators (EPIs) Include both managerial measures about management's efforts to influence environmental performance, such as number of projects and allocated budgets as well as operational measures for results, such as usage rates of energy and water.

environmental sustainability A system of life that allows people, organizations, and governments to meet their current needs without compromising the natural resources available for future generations to meet their future needs. Environmental sustainability rests on the belief that we can coexist with the environment and create minimal or no negative environmental impact. Through environmental sustainability there can be sustainable growth that offers the ability for economic growth and environmental protection to coexist effectively and productively: thus, environmental sustainability practices need not inhibit economic growth, but rather should be viewed as essential to continued economic growth.

EPEAT (Electronic Product Environmental Assessment Tool) A ranking system that helps purchasers in the public and private sectors evaluate, compare, and select desktop computers, notebooks, and monitors based on their environmental attributes.

fossil fuel Any petroleum-based fuel source, such as gasoline, natural gas, and fuel oil.

Gantt charts Bar charts that show activities and durations. Gantt charts are used for scheduling, planning, and managing projects.

global warming Refers to a specific type of climate change, an increased warming of Earth's atmosphere caused by the buildup of man-made gases that trap the sun's heat, causing changes in weather patterns and other effects on a global scale. These effects include global sea level rise, changes in rainfall patterns and frequency, habitat loss, and droughts.

greenhouse gases (GHG)   Gases so named because they contribute to the greenhouse effect due to their high concentrations in the atmosphere. The GHGs of most concern include carbon dioxide (CO_2), methane (CH_4), and nitrous oxide (N_2O).

greenhouse effect   The trapping of heat within the Earth's atmosphere by greenhouse gases such as carbon dioxide, which accumulate in Earth's atmosphere and act as a blanket keeping heat in.

Green business culture   A business environment that considers the environmental consequences of all aspects of its operations via Green initiatives and an environmental sustainability policy.

Green collar   Any kind of employment that involves products or services that are environmentally friendly, such as solar panel installation, weatherizing homes, brewing biofuels, building hybrid cars, and erecting giant wind turbines.

Green computing   The environmentally responsible use of computers and related resources. Such practices include the implementation of energy-efficient central processing units, servers, and peripherals as well as reduced resource consumption and proper disposal of electronic waste (e-waste).

Green data center   A repository for the storage, management, and dissemination of data in which the mechanical, lighting, electrical, and computer systems are designed for maximum energy efficiency and minimum environmental impact. The construction and operation of a Green data center includes advanced technologies and strategies. Building and certifying a Green data center or other facility can be expensive up front, but long-term cost savings can be realized on operations and maintenance.

Green initiative objective assessment   The process of analyzing Green initiative objectives with assessment criteria to determine the outcomes level of success, failure, and compliance. Methods of data collection, surveys, audits, and inspections are used to prepare for outcome analysis. Reports are used to make assessment analysis viewable to internal and external entities and allow for determination of usage of outcome results.

Green networking   The practice of consolidating computing and communication devices and infrastructure, relying more on telecommuting and videoconferencing, and using virtualization to reduce power consumption across the network.

Green reengineering The application of business process reengineering concepts that consider environmental impact, by, for example, proactively redesigning and radically improving manufacturing, packaging, and distribution processes to become more sensitive to the natural environment.

The Green Grid A global consortium dedicated to developing and promoting energy efficiency for data centers and business computing ecosystems by defining meaningful, user-centric models and metrics; promoting the adoption of energy efficient standards, processes, measurement methods, and technologies; and developing standards, measurement methods, processes, and new technologies to improve performance against the defined metrics.

Greenwashing The process by which an organization publicly exaggerates or embellishes the environmental sustainability attributes and practices within its business functions and facilities and/or the environmental benefits of its services and/products. Socially irresponsible and unethical practices are contributors to this act of distrust with the business community and consumers.

Green building A comprehensive process of design and construction that employs techniques to minimize adverse environmental impacts and reduce the energy consumption of a building while contributing to the health and productivity of its occupants; a common metric for evaluating green buildings includes the LEED (Leadership in Energy and Environmental Design) certification.

KPIs (key performance indicators) Metrics that help to assess the present state of a project, objective, or goal. KPIs define a set of values used to measure against and classify different measureable values. They are a component of a scorecard.

Kyoto Protocol An international agreement linked to the United Nations Framework Convention on Climate Change. The major feature of the Kyoto Protocol is that it sets binding targets for 37 industrialized countries and the European Community for reducing greenhouse gas emissions. These amount to an average of 5 percent against 1990 levels over the five-year period 2008 to 2012.

LEED (Leadership in Energy and Environmental Design) An internationally recognized Green building certification system, providing third-party verification that a building or community was designed and built using strategies aimed at improving performance across all the metrics that matter most: energy savings, water efficiency, carbon dioxide emissions reduction, improved indoor environmental quality, and stewardship of resources and sensitivity to their impacts. Developed by the U.S. Green Building Council, LEED provides building owners and operators a concise framework for identifying and implementing practical and measurable Green building design, construction, operations, and maintenance solutions.

milestones Used as markers in a project to set up production points, tasks or moments of synchronization, dates of billing or reporting, and markers or junctions of results.

plan Composed of projects, allocations, simulations, and achievement status.

power management A feature included in many electrical devices (i.e., copiers, computers, monitors, and printers) that turns off the power or switches the system to a standby mode when inactive. Modern laptops and PCs have integrated power management control panels that allow users to fine-tune how quickly a screen turns off. Additionally, power management is offered within computer software (i.e., Microsoft Windows operating systems). Power management features can save individuals and organizations substantial energy costs over time.

power usage effectiveness (PUE) A metric used to determine the energy efficiency of a data center. PUE is determined by dividing the amount of power entering a data center by the power used to run the computer infrastructure within it. PUE is therefore expressed as a ratio, with overall efficiency improving as the quotient decreases toward 1. Data center infrastructure efficiency (DCIE) is the reciprocal of PUE and is expressed as a percentage that improves as it approaches 100%. PUE was created by members of The Green Grid.

process mapping An approach to systematically analyze a particular process. It involves mapping each individual step, or unit operation, undertaken in that process in chronological sequence. Once individual steps are identified, they can be analyzed in more detail. For example, the environmental aspects of a given step can be identified by analyzing its inputs and outputs.

project management office (PMO) Department or group that defines and maintains the standards and processes related to project management within an organization

project   Consists of a temporary endeavor undertaken to create, implement, and/or deploy a new product or service or to modify or change an existing product or service. A project is considered temporary since once its objectives are met, the project team will break up and move on to other projects. The goal of a project is to create something new or unique. A project is composed of tasks and milestones that can be regrouped and interdependent.

recycling   The series of activities, including collection, separation, and processing, by which materials are recovered from the waste stream for use as raw materials in the manufacture of new products.

recyclable   A designation for products or materials that are capable of being recovered from or otherwise diverted from waste streams into an established recycling program.

recycled content   Refers to the amount of recycled materials in a product; typically expressed as a percentage.

renewable energy   Any energy source that is naturally replenished, like that derived from solar, wind, geothermal, or hydroelectric action. Energy produced from the refining of biomass is also often classified as renewable. Coal, oil, and natural gas are finite and nonrenewable sources.

Renewable Energy Credits (RECs)   Otherwise know as Green Tags, Green energy certificates, or tradable renewable certificates. These commodities represent the technology and environmental attributes of electricity generated from renewable resources.

renewable resources   Resources that can be replenished at a rate equal to or greater than their rate of depletion. Examples of renewable resources include corn, trees, and soy-based products.

repurposing   Cleaning or refurbishing that allows a product to be reused again in its current form, thereby extending its useful life.

resource   Represents a person, a group of people, a subcontractor, or the like who can be scheduled on one or several tasks.

resource usage   A curve that indicates how the total capacity of a resource has been used according to the scheduling; this total capacity is divided into unavailability, availability, inefficient allocations, and efficient allocations.

Restriction of Hazardous Substances (RoHS) Directive   Criteria formulated by the European Union in which member states shall ensure that, from July 1, 2006, new electrical and electronic equipment put on the market does not contain any of the six banned substances:

lead, mercury, cadmium, hexavalent chromium, poly-brominated biphenyls (PBB), or polybrominated diphenyl ethers (PBDE), in quantities exceeding maximum concentration values.

scheduling   The process by which project managers assign resources to tasks and timelines.

scorecard   A consolidated visual display of key performance indicators needed to achieve one or more objectives, arranged in a single view with graphical indicators and supporting reports and charts so the information can be reviewed and monitored easily and effectively. A Balanced Scorecard is a type of scorecard.

skill   An additional competence used in relation to the assignment of roles to tasks. Skills allow users to define task requirements and resources more precisely.

stakeholder   An individual or group who potentially can affect and be affected by the activities of a company or organization. Stakeholders have an interest in the success of the organization's environmental sustainability goal and can offer influence and leadership on and with Green initiative programs, products, and services.

standards   Governmental or privately created lists of criteria used to regulate or evaluate the products or behavior or corporations. Standards can play a critical role in stimulating the market and giving companies information to create better products or change corporate behavior. An example is the International Organization for Standardization (ISO).

task   An activity carried out by resources for a definite duration.

task requirement   Composed of one or more roles and skills that are necessary for the achievement of the task.

telecommuting   The use of telecommunication, home office equipment, and the organization's information technology equipment to allow employees to work outside the traditional office or workplace, usually at home or in a mobile situation. Telecommuting can reduce employee travel, thus reducing greenhouse gases, save gasoline usage and associated purchase costs, and reduce urban and air traffic congestion.

videoconferencing   A set of interactive telecommunication technologies that allow employees, sites, and organizations to interact via two-way video and audio transmissions simultaneously. Video transmissions allow for a more realistic and interactive meeting and collaborative experience. Technology can be located on mobile devices, on desktops, and in conference rooms.

virtualization   The creation of a virtual (rather than actual) version of something, such as an operating system, a server, a storage device, or network resources. Implementing server virtualization, for instance, using Microsoft Hyper-V, VMware, or open source competitor Xen can greatly reduce the number of servers required in an enterprise. That translates into reduced energy consumption, less maintenance, and a smaller data center footprint.

waste to energy   The burning of waste in a controlled-environment incinerator to generate steam, heat, or electricity.

About the Author

Carl Speshock is a Senior SQL Server, Business Intelligence and Business Performance Management Consultant for Microsoft Consulting Services and has over 20 years' experience in the IT industry and computer engineering fields. He has been an employee of both Intel and Microsoft corporations. In addition, he served in the United States Marine Corps for 8 years as a Radar Technician with duty throughout the United States and overseas.

He provides training, executive briefings, consultation, and IT speaking engagements to clients, including many Fortune 500 companies from the insurance, petrochemical, oil/gas producing and servicing, mortgage and title, accounting, banking, paper producing, computer manufacturing, industrial engineering, and aerospace industries. Carl has global project experience working on global virtual teams that deliver and implement products and services across the world that have benefits related to environmental sustainability.

He is an MBA-Global Business Management graduate and is currently an IT PhD student with Capella University. Carl has been granted a postgraduate teaching certificate from Capella University and a Data Warehousing Technology certificate from University of California–Berkeley. He is also the author of an IT-related book and several magazine articles.

Carl is a member of professional associations, such as the Society of Petroleum Engineers (SPE), the International Technology Education Association (ITEA), the Association for the Advancement of Computing in Education (AACE), the International Society for Performance Improvement (ISPI) and the Association for Information Systems (AIS)

Carl and his wife and two children have resided in Pearland, Texas, for 15 years.

Index